FIFTY
Quick
IDEAS

TO IMPROVE YOUR

USER
STORIES

by
Gojko Adzic
and
David Evans

FIFTY QUICK IDEAS
TO IMPROVE YOUR USER STORIES

PRINT ISBN: **978-0-9930881-0-0**

Published on: 15 October 2014
Copyright © Neuri Consulting LLP
Authors: Gojko Adzic and David Evans
Copy-editor: Marjory Bisset
Design and layout: Nikola Korac

Published by:
Neuri Consulting LLP
25 Southampton Buildings
London WC2A2AL
United Kingdom

CONTENTS

This book will help you write better stories, spot and fix common issues, split stories so that they are smaller but still valuable, and deal with difficult stuff like cross-cutting concerns, long-term effects and non-functional requirements. Above all, this book will help you achieve the promise of agile and iterative delivery: to ensure that the right stuff gets delivered through productive discussions between delivery team members and business stakeholders.

Who is this book for?

This is a book for anyone working in an iterative delivery environment, doing planning with user stories. The ideas in this book are useful both to people relatively new to user stories and those who have been working with them for years. People who work in software delivery, regardless of their role, will find plenty of tips for engaging stakeholders better and structuring iterative plans more effectively. Business stakeholders working with software teams will discover how to provide better information to their delivery groups, how to set better priorities and how to outrun the competition by achieving more with less software.

Who is this book not for?

This book doesn't cover the basics of stories. We assume that readers know what Card-Conversation-Confirmation means, what INVEST is and how to apply the basic strategies for splitting user stories. This isn't the first book you should read about user stories, if those terms are unfamiliar. There are plenty of good basic books out there, so read them first and then come back. Please don't hate us because we skipped the basics, but there is only so much space in the book and other people cover the basics already well enough.

What's inside?

Unsurprisingly, the book contains exactly fifty ideas. They are grouped into five major parts:

- Creating stories: This part deals with capturing information about stories before they get accepted into the delivery pipeline. You'll find ideas about what kind of information to note down on story cards and how to quickly spot potential problems.
- Planning with stories: This part contains ideas that will help you manage the big-picture view, set milestones and organise long-term work.
- Discussing stories: User stories are all about effective conversations, and this part contains ideas to improve discussions between delivery teams and business stakeholders. You'll find out how to discover hidden assumptions and how to facilitate effective conversations to ensure shared understanding.
- Splitting stories: The ideas in this part will help you deal with large and difficult stories, offering several strategies for dividing them into smaller chunks that will help you learn fast and deliver value quickly.
- Managing iterative delivery: This part contains ideas that will help you work with user stories in the short and mid term, manage capacity, prioritise and reduce scope to achieve the most with the least software.

Each part contains ideas that we've used with teams over the last five or six years to help them manage user stories better and get more value out of iterative delivery. These ideas come from many different contexts, from large investment banks working on internal IT initiatives to small web start-ups shipping consumer software. Software delivery is incredibly contextual, so some stories will apply to your situation, and some won't. Treat all the proposals in this book as experiments – try them out and if they help keep doing them.

JOIN THE CONVERSATION

There is only so much space in a book, and some of the ideas described deserve entire books of their own. We provide plenty of references for further study and pointers for more detailed research in the bibliography at the end of this book. If you're reading this book in electronic form, all the related books and articles are clickable links. If you're reading the book on paper, tapping the text won't help. To save you from having to type in long hyperlinks, we provide all the references online at 50quickideas.com.

If you'd like to get more information on any of the ideas, get additional tips or discuss your experiences with peers, join the Google group 50quickideas.

There is, of course, one more important aspect of user stories: agreeing on the right confirmation criteria for testing. To prevent scope creep, we decided to put ideas about this topic in a separate book. If you are interested, head over to http://50quickideas.com and grab a copy of *Fifty Quick Ideas to Improve Your Tests*.

CREATING STORIES

User stories are often misunderstood as lightweight requirements, given by the business stakeholders to the delivery team. This misunderstanding leads to stories being collected in a task management tool, with a ton of detail written down by business representatives. Except in the very rare case where the business representative is also a technical expert and has a great vision for the product, this division of work prevents organisations from reaping the benefits of user stories.

To make things crystal clear, if a team passively receives documents in a hand-over, regardless of what they are called and whether they are on paper, in a wiki or in a ticketing system, that's not really working with user stories. Organisations with such a process won't get the full benefits of iterative delivery.

User stories imply a completely different model: requirements by collaboration. Hand-overs are replaced by frequent involvement and discussions. When domain and technical knowledge is spread among different people, a discussion between business stakeholders and delivery teams often leads to good questions, options and product ideas. If requirements are just written down and handed over, this discussion does not happen. Even when such documents are called stories, by the

time a team receives them, all the important decisions have already been made.

Effective discussions about user needs, requirements and solutions become critically important with short delivery phases, because there just isn't enough time for anyone to sit down and document everything. Of course, even with longer delivery phases documenting everything rarely works, but people often maintain a pretence of doing it. With delivery phases measured in weeks or days, there isn't enough time to even pretend. When a single person is writing and documenting detailed stories, the entire burden of analysis, understanding and coordination falls on that person. This is not sustainable with a rapid pace of change, and it creates an unnecessary bottleneck. In essence, the entire pipeline moves at the speed of that one person, and she is always too busy.

Try telling stories instead of writing down details. Use physical story cards, electronic ticketing systems and backlog management tools just as reminders for conversations, and don't waste too much time nailing down the details upfront. Engage business stakeholders and delivery team members in a discussion, look at a story from different perspectives and explore options. That's the way to unlock the real benefits of working with user stories.

Key benefits

Discussions allow business representatives not only to explain what they want, but also to ensure that the delivery team members understand this correctly. Misunderstandings between different roles are a major problem with any kind of hand-over. Explaining a story face to face prevents problems from falling through knowledge gaps.

The second benefit is faster analysis. When the entire team is engaged in a discussion, functional gaps, inconsistencies and unclear requirements get discovered faster than when a single person needs to write down the details.

The most important benefit of discussions compared to hand-overs is that they produce better solutions. To be able to design good solutions, people need to know business plans and opportunities, understand the problem domain, have in-depth knowledge of technical constraints and an awareness of potential new technologies. Engaging a group of people in analysis from different perspectives helps the team benefit from shared knowledge.

How to make it work

There are several common reasons for writing down detailed stories. Most of these needs can be met without document hand-overs. Here are the most common excuses:

- When regulatory requirements or the political environment require formal sign-offs, written details serve as a record of what was approved.
- When different business stakeholders have to agree or approve plans, having something written to send out. is useful. Geographically distributed organisations often have this need.
- If stories depend on the specialist knowledge of people who aren't available to participate in story discussions, written details are a good way to transfer their knowledge.
- Where third-party dependencies or legacy systems require time-consuming analysis and investigation, involving the entire team in that would be a waste of time. Written details are a good way to capture the outcomes of the investigation.

The most common excuse for handing over documents is insisting on formal approval of scope. Without going into whether formal approval is right or wrong, if you must have it, postpone the sign-off until after story discussions. Get each story signed off as you discuss it. We've worked with several teams in regulated environments where due process demanded that a business sponsor approves scope. In such cases, business sponsors have signed off on specifications with examples produced as a result of story refinement and analysis discussions.

If the final scope has to be approved by several different business stakeholders, have the conversation a few days before officially starting to implement a story, and then coordinate with the stakeholders. For example, a team we worked with in an insurance company needed to get the details approved by all country managers, so they discussed stories a week ahead of the iteration. Their product owner then collected the results of the discussions, refined them into specifications, and sent them out to all business stakeholders to agree.

Effective teams with third party dependencies, or those that rely on external specialist knowledge, generally dedicate one or two people to investigate those dependencies a week or two before starting a story. The results of the investigations are a great starting point for the story analysis discussions.

Some teams analyse stories twice as a group: once a week or two ahead of the iteration to collect open questions and focus the upfront investigation, and the second time just ahead of the iteration to communicate and agree on the details. In such cases the details are often collected in the same task management tool as the stories, but teams treat them only as notes to start a discussion, not as formal requirements for sign-off.

DON'T WORRY TOO MUCH ABOUT STORY FORMAT

There is plenty of advice out there about different formats of story cards. Some argue that putting the business value statement first focuses delivery on business value, some argue that 'So that I can' is a much better start than 'In order to', and we've heard passionate presentations about how 'I suggest' is better than 'I want'. We're going to swim against the current here and offer a piece of controversial advice: don't worry too much about the format!

There are three main reasons why you shouldn't trouble yourselves too much with the exact structure of a user story, *as long as the key elements are there*:

- A story card is ideally just a token for a conversation. Assuming the information on the card is not false, any of the formats is good enough to start the discussion. If the information on the card is false, they are all equally bad.

- Although we've read and heard plenty of arguments for different card types, there wasn't a single clear proof that choosing one format over another improved team performance by a significant amount. Show us where reordering statements on a story card improved profit by more than 1% and we'll talk.

- As an industry, we love syntax wars. If you ever need proof that IT is full of obsessive-compulsive types, look up on the web the best indentation level, the undoubted superiority of tabs over spaces, or the most productive position for curly braces. Beyond the obvious argument about personal preference, there is value in choosing one standard way for writing code for the entire team, regardless of what gets chosen. But code is a long-term artefact, and user stories are discussion reminders that have served their purpose after a conversation. So the standardisation argument does not really apply here.

The Connextra card template ('As a... I want ... So that') is a great structure for a discussion token. It proposes a deliverable and puts it in the context of a stakeholder benefit, which helps immensely with the discussion. But that's not the only way to start a good conversation. As long as the story card stimulates a good discussion, it serves its purpose. Write down who wants something and why they want it in any way you see fit, and do something more productive with the rest of your time than filling in a template just because you have to. For example, make sure that the person in question is actually a stakeholder, and that they actually want what the card says.

An interesting take on this is to experiment with different formats to see if something new comes out during discussion. For example:

- Name stories early, add details later
- Avoid spelling out obvious solutions
- Think about more than one stakeholder who would be interested in the item – this opens up options for splitting the story
- Use a picture instead of words
- Ask a question

Chris Matts, one of the agile business analysis thought-leaders, has a nice example:

My favourite story card had the Japanese Kanji characters Ni and Hon (the name for Japan in native script) on it. Nothing else. It was the card for Japanese language translation.

When we wrote this, Gojko was working on a product milestone that was mostly about helping users obtain information more easily. Most user stories for the milestone were captured as examples of questions people would be able to answer, such as: 'How much potential cash is there in blocked projects?' and 'What is the average time spent on sales?'. These are perfectly good stories, as they fulfil both important roles nicely: they allow delivery teams to schedule things and they spark a good discussion. Each question is just an example, and leads to a discussion on the best way of providing information to users to answer a whole class of related questions. Forcing the stories into a three-clause template just for the sake of it would not give the team any more benefit, and it might even mislead the discussion as it would limit it to only one solution.

Key benefits

Letting go of a template, and trying out different formats, can help to shake up the discussion. This also helps to prevent fake stories. Following a template just for the sake of it is a great way to build a cargo cult. This is where stories such as 'As a trader I want to trade because I want to trade' come from, as well as 'As a System I want the ... report'.

By trying out different formats, you might wake up some hidden creativity in the team, or discover a different perspective during the discussion about a story.

How to make it work

The one thing you really have to do to make this work is to avoid feature requests. If you have only a short summary on a card, it must not be a solution without context. So, 'How much potential cash is in blocked projects?' is a valid summary, but a 'Cash report' isn't. The potential cash question actually led to a pop-up dialog that presented a total of cash by status for any item in the document, not to a traditional tabular report.

Focus on the problem statement, the user side of things, instead of on the software implementation. The way to avoid trouble is to describe a behaviour change as the summary. For example 'Get a profit overview faster', or 'Manage deliveries more accurately'.

Bill Wake's INVEST set of user story characteristics has two conflicting forces. *Independent* and *valuable* are often difficult to reconcile with *small*. The value of software is a vague and esoteric concept in the domain of business users, but task size is under the control of a delivery team, so many teams end up choosing size over value. This results in technical stories, that is, stories that don't really produce any outcome, and a disconnect between what the team is pushing out and what the business sponsors really care about.

Many delivery teams also implicitly assume that something has value just because business users are asking for it, so they don't question it. Robert Brinkerhoff, in *Systems Thinking in Human Resource Development*, argues that valuable initiatives produce an observable change in someone's way of working. This principle is a great way to start a conversation on the value of a story

or to unblock a sticky situation. In essence, translating Brinkerhoff's idea to software means that it's not enough to describe just someone's behaviour, but we should aim to describe a change in that behaviour instead. This trick is particularly useful with user stories that have an overly generic value statement, or where the value statement is missing.

We recently worked with a team that was struggling to describe acceptance criteria for a user story that was mostly about splitting a background process into two. The story was perceived to be of value because the business stakeholders had asked for it. It was a strange situation, because the story was purely technical – a division of a background task. The success criterion was deceivingly simple – check that we have two jobs instead of one – so the team was worried that there was more to this than met the eye. The value statement was 'being able to import contacts'. The problem was that the users were able to import contacts already, and they would still be able to import contacts after the story was done – there was no real success criterion. We tried to capture the value not just as a behaviour, but as a change in that behaviour, and the discussion suddenly took a much more productive turn. Some people argued that splitting the background process would allow users to import contacts faster, but the total time for a split task would be the same. So either the solution was wrong, or the assumed value was incorrect. Digging deeper into what would be different after the story was delivered, we discovered that users could not import large contact files easily. Imported data was going directly into the database, where it was processed in several steps synchronously. For large files, this process took longer than the allowed time for an HTTP request, so the users saw an error on the screen. They would have to re-upload the file and wait to see if it had been processed. We finally identified the change as 'being able to upload larger sets of contacts faster', and this opened a discussion on several potential solutions. One was to just store the uploaded file on the server and complete the HTTP request, letting the user go and do other things, while the same job as before picks up the file in the background and processes it. It was a better solution than the one in the original request because it did not depend on the speed of the background process, and it was also easier and faster to implement.

In addition, understanding the expected behaviour changes allowed the team to set a good acceptance criterion for the user story. They could test that a large file upload completes within the HTTP request timeout limit, instead of just checking for the number of background tasks.

Key benefits

Capturing a behaviour change makes a story measurable from a business perspective, and this always opens up a good discussion. In our example, once we knew that a change was about uploading larger sets of contacts faster, two questions immediately popped up: how much larger, and how much faster? The right solution completely depended on these two factors. Were we talking about megabytes or gigabytes? Were we talking about speeding something up by a small percentage, or by an order of magnitude?

Answering questions like these helps to determine whether the proposed solution is appropriate, inadequate or over the top. Describing the behaviour change sets the context which allows a delivery teams to propose better solutions.

Describing expected changes allows teams to assess whether a story succeeds from a business perspective once it is delivered. Even if the story passes all technical and functional tests, if it fails to produce the expected behaviour change, it is not complete. This might lead the business sponsors to suggest more stories. By the same token, if there are several stories all aimed at the same behaviour change and the first one achieves more than planned, then the other stories can be thrown out of the plan – they are not needed any more.

A measurable behaviour change makes stories easier to split, because there is one more dimension to discuss. For example, if the behaviour change is 'import contacts 20% faster', offering a small subset of functionality that speeds up importing by 5% is still valuable.

How to make it work

Try to quantify expected changes – a good change is one that is observable and measurable. Effectively, once you have identified a change, ask 'How much?' Even if you do not end up measuring it, capturing how much change is expected will help you discuss the proposed solutions. If discrete values are difficult to set, aim for ranges. For example, instead of '10% faster', ask about the minimum that would make a behaviour change valuable, and what would make it over the top. Then set the range somewhere in between.

Teams sometimes struggle to do this for new capabilities. If the capability is not there yet, then 'Start to' or 'Stop doing' are valid behaviour changes. Then you can discuss what exactly 'Start to' means. For example, a team we worked with had several weeks of work planned to enable traders to sell a new category of products, but it turned out that they could start to trade by logging purchase orders in Excel. The Excel solution did not deliver the final speed or capacity they needed, but traders started selling several months sooner than if they had to wait for the full big-bang deployment to production, and this had immense business value for the company.

16

Just as every story should describe a behaviour change that represents the business value (the 'why') of the story, it should also be clear about the change a team needs to make to software (the 'what') in order to bring about or enable that change in user behaviour.

When a story is first proposed, the exact nature of what should be changed in the system might be a matter of choice between several design options, and it is right and proper to defer commitment on a solution until we are clear about the intended outcome. But once we have settled on the best solution, the story description should be clear about exactly how the system functionality or business rules will differ between now and when the story is implemented. (Note that this is not about specifying implementation details in the story, just the difference in observable system outputs.)

If we are building a new product, it may be that most stories are about creating new features from scratch. But for established products undergoing steady evolution and maintenance, most stories are about making changes to existing features. Even if a story does add a whole new feature, there are inevitably changes to existing system behaviour to weave the new feature into the product. In each case, we need to be clear about the scope of all the changes required to consider the story done.

Often, the short description of a story leaves a lot of ambiguity about what the scope of the change will be. Even when it is being discussed face to face, it may not be clear to everyone what the full implications would be of taking on the story. It is important to bottom out the discussions around the specifics of how the system behaviour is going to change.

A typical story description includes a clause describing the 'what' of the story, usually in the 'I want...' part of the story template. Even if the required system behaviour is accurately described, the amount of work required from the team to implement it depends on how much it differs from the current system behaviour, and this might not be clear to everyone. In many cases we also need an 'instead of' clause to follow the 'I want'.

For example, imagine we had the following story for a financial trading system: *'In order to continue trading while not breaching regulations, As a trader, I want a warning message when the total volume of trades reaches within 10% of my daily trading limit.'* The behaviour change that we want to influence is to have traders maximise their trading opportunities without exceeding regulatory limits. The feature we need in order to support this behaviour change is a warning to the trader when they are getting close to the limit.

However, unless we are very familiar with what the relevant part of the system does already, we can't tell on the face of it whether this is a major change or not. Consider some of these possibilities:

- Is there already any concept of daily volume limits in place? If not, this story has to build a lot of new things, and would be relatively complex to implement.
- Does the system already have daily limits which it prevents traders from exceeding? If so, much of the existing logic could be reused to trigger the required warning, and it would be only a moderate change.
- Is there already a warning in place, but triggered at a different point? Changing the warning threshold to 10% would be a very simple change.

The point is that the description of the required feature alone, even if complete and accurate, is not enough to indicate how complex the story is to implement. We also need to know how much it differs from the current behaviour.

Key benefits

When developers and testers are discussing a story, either to estimate its complexity, identify technical implementation tasks or design acceptance test cases, it is invaluable to have a concisely expressed description of the expected changes. When the scope of the change is clearly delineated, the team is more likely to reach a quick agreement on how much work there is to do.

Clarifying the change is a valid and useful step in the refinement of the story. In some cases the process of identifying the extent of the change can help in splitting larger stories.

How to make it work

Start the discussion by adding another clause to the story template, starting with 'Whereas currently...' or 'Instead of...'. The wording of this phrase should make as clear as possible the contrast between what we already have and what is needed.

Another option is to follow the 'I want' phrase with a verb that highlights the new action or behaviour. Test whether the verb is the right one by asking negative questions. If the change is expressed as *'I want to access the reports using a mobile device'* you can ask *'Is it the case that you can't access the reports at the moment?'* If the answer comes back as *'Well, I can already access the reports, but I have to use the website instead of the application'* then the verb is the wrong one. It would be better to say *'I want to use a native application when I access the reports'*.

In the trading volume example, applying these techniques might result in the story being amended as follows: *'In order to notify traders they are nearing trading volume limits, the system will warn traders when the total volume reaches within 10% of the daily trading limit, whereas currently there is no warning message and trading continues until the daily limit is exceeded at which point all trades are blocked'*.

A common description for stories is that they are small chunks of work that can be implemented within an iteration, yet still bring some value. This description is likely to be the cause of a range of communication problems between many teams and their business users. Because teams primarily aim to create something small, instead of something valuable, they end up with a bunch of small stories that are too disconnected from what business sponsors care about. Such stories are seldom deployable on their own to production, so they rarely provide opportunity for serious business feedback. Ultimately, this can lead to business users not really caring about individual stories, and waiting for a larger batch of work to be ready for testing, undermining the value of iterative delivery.

In *Adapt*, a wonderful book on adaptive planning in everything from civil engineering to the military and the economy, author Tim Harford explains how linear plans rarely work due to influences beyond our control. Today's IT industry is a poster child for most of the problems he describes. Even with the best intentions, our plans might not work out as expected – users can often decide whether to use, misuse or completely ignore what we deliver, technical or business dependencies can make a solution incomplete, changes in external circumstances and third party systems can make a proposed solution invalid or obsolete. Instead of bearing the consequences of unexpected changes, Harford suggests turning a shifting landscape into a competitive advantage. One of the key aspects is to treat plans as series of survivable experiments. Stories are potentially a great fit for this approach, but we have to conceptually change how we think about them.

Stories shouldn't be small because they need to fit into an iteration, but because the world shouldn't end just because a story turns out to be wrong. Stories are based on assumptions about business value, and those assumptions might turn out to be right or wrong. The key questions for story sizing shouldn't be about the iteration length, but about how much business stakeholders want to invest in learning whether a proposed change will actually give them what they assumed.

In markets with a high degree of certainty, where business sponsors can perfectly predict the future, where there is no competition, where the entire ecosystem is under strict control and the end-users are a captive audience whose personal opinions have no influence on the outcome, iterative delivery simply doesn't bring any business value. If any of these dimensions is not under your control, iterative delivery with survivable experiments can be a great way to turn unplanned changes in circumstances into competitive advantage. Stories have to be small, but fitting into an iteration should be a consequence, not a cause. It's far better to sell them on value instead of size.

Key benefits

Small user stories can help product managers discover what really needs to be built without rushing too far forward under unvalidated assumptions, and help business sponsors manage their investment in software and get the most out of it. That's how we should sell them, not as small chunks of work.

By approaching stories as survivable experiments we can shift the focus from technical complexity to expected outcomes and learning. This prevents technical stories, stories that are too small to go live and stories that business sponsors don't care about.

Looking at stories as survivable experiments also solves many problems around story splitting and sizing. If a story is too big, which effectively means the potential cost of the experiment is too high, we can look at alternative ways of learning about something instead of just trying to slice the story.

Small, survivable stories help business sponsors manage their investment in software and get the most out of it.

How to make it work

If you have a big chunk of work, identify underlying assumptions and think about the easiest way of proving or disproving them. Design experiments around those assumptions and turn them into user stories. Use the experiments to build up the foundation, so that the rest of the big picture can be delivered with small iterative improvements.

For example, launching a completely new mobile application to increase user engagement is a huge piece of work. It would depend on a host of third parties including mobile networks, application store operators and many others. It would depend on discovering and satisfying local user interests, which will differ by location. One of the assumptions in such cases is typically that a mobile-optimised user interface would keep users engaged for longer compared to a desktop-optimised website. A way to prove or disprove that assumption might be to direct a small group of customers to a mobile-optimised web homepage when they use a mobile device. If this experiment would be too costly, then it can be further narrowed down by selecting the test group so that the relevant homepage can be generated more easily, for example, users in a single city. If that piece of work is still too big, the content can be limited in time. A simple user story could deliver a static, manually crafted homepage, limiting access to only the chosen location, but with some good analytics that could prove or disprove the assumptions. Further user stories can then bring more locations into the experiment iteratively (for example, new static homepages for other cities), or reduce the maintenance cost for the chosen city (automating content-building). The content automation is likely to be a small slice, but will also ultimately be useful for the final mobile application. Similar small experiments can be planned for other underlying assumptions.

One of the biggest advantages of user stories is getting delivery teams to think from the perspectives of users. Instead of purely focusing on how to build something, delivery teams consider how their products will be used. This is central to the user story technique – hence the name. Yet the vast majority of stories we've seen in the wild refer to a completely generic customer segment, very often starting literally with 'As a user...'

In a horrible case of mistaken identity, a placeholder on a template became an acceptable value, and teams started using a mythical generic user to justify scope creep. A generic user role can never provide a useful context for discussion. Without considering a particular user segment, it's impossible to decide whether the proposed solution is the right one, or if it's just unnecessary scope creep. Unless we think about a narrow

target group, it's impossible to effectively plan releases and measure impacts or even discuss completeness.

Using generic roles is often a get-out-of-jail-free card for people who want to push in pet features, or unjustified scope. For example, a team we recently worked with had a story 'As a user I want to log in through social networks in order not to remember another username and password'. The story checklist originally involved Facebook, Twitter, LinkedIn, Google+ and OpenID, and all those would become individual stories later on. Because it was not clear who was the mythical user, the stakeholders clearly thought that the more networks the team could integrate the better. Someone even found a third-party service that would allow twenty or so social networks to be integrated instantly. The service would be cheap at first, but bring significant cost at scale. It was difficult to judge whether using the third party service was a better choice than integrating with individual networks, until the team challenged the generic role. The two major groups that would really benefit from this story were both from the educational world: teachers and students in schools. This pushed the discussion towards integrating only with Google accounts. Google accounts include Google Apps for Education, very popular in educational institutions, and would allow anyone with a Google Mail account to sign in as well. LinkedIn is a network for professionals and it wasn't particularly popular with the newly understood target audience. Although Facebook and Twitter are popular with the new target group, many schools actually block those sites from school networks, so integrating those would probably be a waste of time. By challenging a generic user role and considering a concrete customer segment, the team was able to significantly reduce unnecessary scope and make important product management decisions more easily (no need to buy a third party service).

Avoid 'as a user' statements like the plague. Avoid overly generic customer segment descriptions of any kind. Don't just aim to fill in a placeholder in a story template, identify and describe user segments that will help you facilitate productive discussion of needs and solutions.

Key benefits

Focusing stories on a particular customer segment helps to kick-start useful conversations about user stories. Clear and accurate descriptions of user roles help to identify needs and remove unnecessary complexity. Once you understand who will use the product you're building, it becomes possible to compare different solution options, offer alternatives or even discard features that won't fit.

In addition, well-defined user roles are crucial when you want to implement good product management and planning strategies, for example splitting stories by narrowing down segments, or prioritising impacts on customer groups.

How to make it work

For internal IT or enterprise projects, try to identify the actual people who will be using the target system, and investigate how work is divided. Different departments or areas of focus will help you identify useful user segments.

For consumer systems, good starting points are user personae, described in many good books including Alan Cooper's *Inmates are Running the Asylum*. Another nice reference is the persona checklist presented by Stephen Wendel in *Designing for Behavior Change*:
- Prior experience with action
- Prior experience with similar products and channels
- Relationship with company or organisation
- Existing motivation
- Physical, psychological or economic impediments to action

This checklist is great because it enables teams to identify quickly different groups of users based on five important aspects. Note that the term 'action' in Wendel's system refers to the activity that is assisted or managed by the software product, which maps to the benefit of a story ('in order to...').

An alternative approach is to group users by common behaviours. Market research is often a good start for defining customer groups, because they structure surveys by needs and behaviours. A great example of this is the *Anatomy of a Live Music Fan* survey published by BandsInTown (see the bibliography).

EVALUATE ZONE OF CONTROL AND SPHERE OF INFLUENCE

In *The Logical Thinking Process*, H. William Dettmer talks about three different areas of systems:

- The *zone of control* includes all those things in a system that we can change on our own.
- The *sphere of influence* includes activities that we can impact, but can't exercise full control over.
- The *external environment* includes the elements over which we have no influence.

These three system areas, and the boundaries between them, provide a very useful perspective on what a delivery team can hope to achieve with user stories.

A good guideline is that the user need of a story ('In order to...') should ideally be in the sphere of influence of the delivery team, and the deliverable ('I want...') should ideally be in their zone of control. This is not a 100% rule and there are valid exceptions, but if a story does not fit into this pattern it should be investigated.

When the user need of a story is in the zone of control of the delivery group, the story is effectively a task without risk, which should raise alarm bells. There are three common scenarios: The story might be fake, micro-story or misleading.

Fake stories are those about the needs of delivery team members. For example, 'As a QA, in order to test faster, I want the database server restarts to be automated'.

Micro-stories are what you get when a large business story is broken down into very small pieces, so that some small parts no longer carry any risk – they are effectively stepping stones to something larger. Such stories are

OK, but it's important to track the whole hierarchy and measure the success of the micro-stories based on the success of the larger piece. If the combination of all those smaller pieces still fails to achieve the business objective, it might be worth taking the whole hierarchy out or revisiting the larger piece.

Misleading stories describe a solution and not the real user need. One case we came across recently was 'As a back-office operator, in order to run reports faster, I want the customer reporting database queries to be optimised'. At first glance, this seemed like a nice user story – it even included a potentially measurable change in someone's behaviour. However, the speed of report execution is pretty much in the zone of control of the delivery team, which prompted us to investigate further. We discovered that the operator asking for the change was looking for discrepancies in customer information. He ran several different reports just to compare them manually. Because of the volume of data and the systems involved, he had to wait around for 20 to 30 minutes for the reports, and then spend another 10 to 20 minutes loading the different files into Excel and comparing them. We could probably have decreased the time needed for the first part of that job significantly, but the operator would still have had to spend time comparing information. Then we traced the request to something outside our zone of control. Running reports faster helped the operator to compare customer information, which helped him to identify discrepancies (still within our control potentially), and then to resolve them by calling the customers and cleaning up their data. Cleaning up customer data was outside our zone of control, we could just influence it by providing information quickly. This was a nice place to start discussing the story and its deliverables. We rephrased the story to 'In order to resolve customer data discrepancies faster...' and implemented a web page that quickly compared different data sources and almost instantly displayed only the differences. There was no need to run the lengthy reports, the database software was more than capable of zeroing in on the differences very quickly. The operator could then call the customers and verify the information.

When the deliverable is outside the zone of control of the delivery team, there are two common situations: the expectation is completely unrealistic, or the story is not completely actionable by the delivery group.

The first case is easy to deal with – just politely reject it. The second case is more interesting. Such stories might need the involvement of an external specialist, or a different part of the organisation. For example, one of our clients was a team in a large financial organisation where configuration changes to message formats had to be executed by a specialist central team. This, of course, took a lot of time and coordination. By doing the zone of control/sphere of influence triage on stories, we quickly identified those that were at risk of being delayed. The team started on them quickly, so that everything would be ready for the specialists as soon as possible.

Key benefits

The concepts of the zone of control and sphere of influence are crucial for systems thinking. By inspecting stories that fall outside the usual pattern, we can identify root causes of problems and work on them, instead of just dealing with the symptoms.

How to make it work

The system boundaries vary depending on viewpoint, so consider them from the perspective of the delivery team.

If a story does not fit into the expected pattern, raise the alarm early and consider re-writing it. Throw out or replace fake and misleading stories. Micro-stories aren't necessarily bad, but going so deep into detail is probably an overkill for anything apart from short-term plans. If you discover micro-stories on medium-term or long-term plans, it's probably better to replace a whole group of related stories with one larger item.

If you discover stories that are only partially actionable by your team, consider splitting them into a part that is actionable by the delivery group, and a part that needs management intervention or coordination.

PUT A 'BEST BEFORE' DATE ON STORIES

Handing time-constrained changes is one of the major challenges of planning with flexible scope. This is often a blind spot for teams working with user stories, especially if they have many stakeholders. Time-bound items might start as low priority, but as the deadline approaches they become more critical. When time constraints are not clearly specified, such items are difficult to spot and manage until they become emergencies.

A team we recently worked with had to implement several new reports to support an upcoming change in regulations. The financial controller asked for them about six months ahead of the deadline, but as other things were always more important, the reports never got to the top of the list. A week before the regulation change, the financial controller panicked and the whole team went into fire-fighting mode. Another stakeholder caused something similar two weeks later. Looking at their planned and actual work over the previous six months, we discovered many similar cases. The team felt that the business stakeholders changed priorities randomly, which was causing almost constant fire-fighting. The business stakeholders felt that the team was not productive enough, and that they did not care about business priorities. The issue was, as in most similar cases, not with incompetence on either side but with communication.

EXPIRED!

Instead of blindly accepting stories into the backlog and forgetting about them until a stakeholder screams, the team started to investigate timing constraints early on. When proposing a story, a stakeholder would have to specify the 'best before' date as well. This was effectively a signal that the work required by that story would become an emergency one week before the date. Stories with expiry dates were clearly separated from the rest of the backlog, which allowed the team to slot in such stories into earlier iterations, dealing with them at a sustainable pace. Some stakeholders realised that this was an easy way to cheat the system and get higher priority for their needs, so the scheduling system was slightly adjusted to prohibit 'rotten fruit' – stories which would expire almost immediately.

One of the biggest benefits of working with user stories is allowing stakeholders to frequently change priorities and adjust scope. But this shouldn't be used as an excuse to ignore known time constraints, which will only lead to a lot of fire-fighting later. Flexible scope is great when you need to react quickly, but frequent fire-fighting is unsustainable. When a team is reacting to an emergency, other work suffers and quick and dirty changes cause a lot of technical debt. In most cases that we've seen, someone knew about the upcoming deadline months in advance, but this was not clearly communicated. There really is no reason for such stories to become so critical as to cause an emergency. They can be handled at a sustainable pace.

In order to avoid unnecessary pressure and self-inflicted emergencies, check whether there is an expiry date when new user stories are proposed. Write down the best before date on those stories and make it visually obvious that they are special so that you can manage them separately.

Key benefits

A clear expiry date allows teams to manage time-constrained stories before they become urgent. This reduces emergencies, context switching, technical debt and allows the teams to handle real emergencies more effectively.

Sooner or later, your delivery team will have a genuine emergency to deal with: a story that must be implemented straight away. An urgent story is like an ambulance in a traffic jam. Turning on a siren and rushing through only works if most of the cars on the road are not ambulances as well. Making sure everyone is aware of deadlines and works to them removes most of the noise and lets the team deal with genuine emergencies better.

How to make it work

The most important action is to ask about potential deadlines and clearly specify them when items come into the plan. It is also a very good idea to mark those items visually so that they can be identified quickly. Kanban popularised delivery plans with several classes of service, where different types of work can be assigned different service levels. If you are using a flow-based process, it might be a good idea to create a separate lane on your board for fixed-date items, so you can clearly monitor them. Other effective ways of separating out fixed-date items are using different shaped or coloured cards, or having a calendar next to the planning board and fixing items onto the calendar several weeks before the deadline.

Generally, it is a good idea to require that stakeholders propose time-constrained stories a certain length of time before the deadline, much in the way that airplane companies require passengers to check in at least 30 minutes before their flight. For example, agree on a service level where a best before date has to be at least one month after the date when a story is initially proposed. This stops the 'rotten fruit' stories from coming into the backlog.

Don't aim to put a best before date on all stories, otherwise everything can become an emergency. Keep this only for stories with a genuine timing constraint, so you can manage them differently from the others. Teams with many stakeholders will probably find it useful to limit the number of stories with an expiry date, either as a percentage of the active backlog or the total number.

If you use impact maps, put time constraints on higher-level impacts instead of individual stories. This will help with prioritisation of impacts, but also with managing entire groups of related stories.

25

PLANNING WITH STORIES

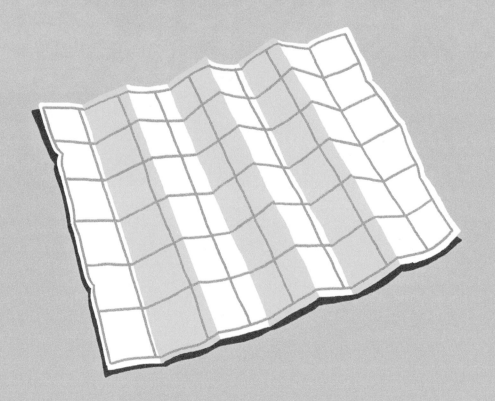

SET DEADLINES FOR ADDRESSING MAJOR RISKS

Planning with user stories, if done well, puts business stakeholders well and truly in the driving seat for decisions on software delivery. It enables teams to deliver value frequently, react to market opportunities and outrun the competition. Most of the tips in this book are about delivering value sooner. But in this section, we'd like to warn against a potential pitfall with focusing too much on this.

A few years ago Gojko audited a legacy migration initiative, where the delivery team, wanting to be helpful, encouraged the business stakeholders to replan and reprioritise frequently. The decision-makers constantly chose small wins and low-hanging fruit. After a year and a half of work, data migration had never come to the top of the list of priorities, largely because it was a big, messy, risky problem. With the budget almost spent and small wins not really providing the return on investment expected from the legacy migration, the project was canned.

Perhaps an even better example of delivering small increments while losing the big picture is the FBI Sentinel project, which cost 451 million USD and almost failed. In *Why the FBI Can't Build a Case Management System*, Jerome Israel highlights one of the biggest risks of iterative delivery. After the first phase of the Sentinel project, the FBI wanted more visibility so they required the contractor to start delivering software frequently. As a safeguard, they created a strong programme management department. During Phase 2, the programme managers had bi-monthly meetings with senior FBI stakeholders, showing status charts. They even had a project thermometer, which captured the overall status in red, yellow or green. For two years, the thermometer always showed yellow trending towards green. In October 2009, the contractor missed its deadline for delivery of Phase 2, and all the critical problems 'came crashing down on the project'. An independent audit of the project concluded that there were more than '10,000 inefficiencies'. In *The Lean Mindset*, Tom and Mary Poppendieck comment on that study, saying that due to the pressure to demonstrate progress, development turned towards easy tasks and always postponed serious risks. The project management approach focused on tracking activity, and not on addressing risks. Although the Sentinel project did not employ user stories in the first two phases, this example is quite illustrative of the situation we see often with teams working on stories. (The Phase 2 failure caused them to adopt agile methods eventually and the story has a happy ending.)

Both examples illustrate how having to make frequent deliveries makes teams focus on short-term wins and neglect long-term risks, until the work becomes completely unsustainable. This is caused not only by the pressure to deliver but also by doing progress reports mostly by tracking activity. Prioritisation is a big problem with user stories, especially if business stakeholders do not have experience with iterative planning. Small, easy wins always get prioritised over difficult tasks. It's like children choosing between chocolate and broccoli. User stories are split to avoid risky areas, and at some point the celling comes crashing down. To avoid falling into this trap, delivery teams should work with stakeholders to set explicit deadlines for addressing major risks at a sustainable pace.

Key benefits

Having an explicit plan to deal with big risks allows stakeholders and the delivery team to strike the right balance between short-term business wins and long-term sustainability.

It's a good idea to plan deadlines that deal with risks as decision points for incremental investment. This helps to prevent difficult and risky work from being constantly postponed and replaced with small short-term wins.

How to make it work

At the Scandinavian Developer Conference in 2011, Alistair Cockburn suggested periodically shifting gears during delivery and alternating between 'paying to learn' (addressing major risks) and 'paying to get business value'. Cockburn advised that in earlier stages, the focus should be more on addressing risks than on building value. His summary was 'Develop for business value – once the risks are down'.

For new product development, you can use the *Lean Analytics* stages of growth model to decide which risks to address and when to switch between delivering value and addressing risks as the product moves through the different stages. For internal IT initiatives, identify major risks and decide when such areas need to be clarified so that stakeholders can make sustainable planning decisions.

One potential strategy is to plan for addressing risks with learning stories, and put a 'best before' date on them. It is also a good idea to agree upfront what kind of deliverables need to be in place to show that the risks have been addressed: full implementation of the relevant piece of software, a working prototype, or just a conceptual design.

Creating a hierarchical backlog can also stop the team and stakeholders from turning delivery into a stream of consciousness and never dealing with big risks. Once a hierarchy is in place, stakeholders can prioritise at a level higher than stories, for example by picking impacts. Putting deadlines on items that address risks can help to balance out risk mitigation and delivery of value, as delivering stories with major impacts is likely to require both.

As an aside, please don't use activity metrics such as velocity or burn-down scope to measure progress. They only show that people have been busy, not that they were working on the right things or even producing something valuable. Activity metrics are great to measure whether the team is working well together or not, but they can't show real progress. Measuring progress with activity creates a completely wrong set of incentives for prioritisation. Instead, create a model for expected business value delivery and report progress towards it.

One of the deepest pitfalls of fake iterative delivery is story card hell, nicely described by Jim Shore in 2005:

Story card hell is when you have 300 story cards and you have to keep track of them all... When you have 300 cards, you lose the ability to understand what they mean.

Unfortunately, almost a decade later, we often meet teams who have ended up in that limbo. Story card hell is dangerous because it provides an illusion that the process is working iteratively, whereas in fact the teams are following a detailed plan set months ago. Three key problems arising from this are:

- The delivery team wastes a horrible amount of time tracking and managing unnecessary items – time that could have been invested much more wisely. Having to manage all this information often puts a lot of strain on product managers, who then do not have enough time to deal with day-to-day activities.

- When market opportunities change the business stakeholders are faced with a serious dilemma. Aligning the plan to meet the changed circumstances would lead to throwing away a lot of work sunk into estimation and breaking commitments. Keeping the plan would lead to delivering outdated or useless features or delaying work on something more important.

- It's very easy to hide scope creep and unnecessary work in a pile of several dozen items. It becomes very difficult to challenge the value and goal of individual items in such a big pile, which means that it's much more likely that the team will waste time doing the wrong things.

Most people that fall into this trap are pressured to do it by their business stakeholders. On one hand, if you want to run an iterative process, it's pretty much pointless to define the entire scope up front. On the other hand, business stakeholders – especially those responsible for budgeting – want to keep track of costs and push for detailed estimates. We'll deal with the issue of estimates later, but for now let's deal with the planning aspect of this problem.

One of Elisabeth Hendrickson's ideas that we like the most is that people who ask for control often really want visibility. Small user stories, deliverable within an iteration, are great for providing low-level process visibility. They are useless for a big-picture view, though. This lack of big-picture visibility is a key reason why business stakeholders push for detailed estimates and commitments on dozens or hundreds of stories upfront.

This is where asteroids come in. Not the real ones, but white circular shapes, moving quickly on 1980s TV screens, connected to small furnaces labelled ATARI. Space fighter pilots would shoot at asteroids and break them into smaller pieces, then break those rocks further until they were so small that a laser shot vaporised them. Touch an asteroid with your plane, and the game is over. The asteroids game is immense fun. But it's also quite educational from the perspective of iterative planning with user stories.

Like most other good visual metaphors for agile product management, this one comes from Jeff Patton. A sure way to lose the asteroids game is to break up all the big rocks early. This produces a ton of small asteroids flying all over the place, and makes it impossible for the pilot to navigate without crashing. The way to win is to pick off one large asteroid at a time, keeping the number of mid-size asteroids on the screen low enough to be able to navigate, and to vaporise smaller asteroids as soon as they form. Managing the number of on-screen asteroids in different size categories is crucial. Small ones are

the most important, but at the same time, it would be unwise to take your eyes off the big asteroids.

Similarly, a sure way to lose the agile planning game is to break up all the big items into small ones, so that the team cannot navigate and change course any more. But you can't work only on the big items, because you would not be able to plan effectively. The story card hell problem starts when a team only has one level of abstraction in their backlog – when the backlog becomes linear. The solution is to make the backlog hierarchical.

Try to divide your plan into several tiers, and then avoid breaking down a higher-level item until you complete all the relevant lower-level stories for the previous higher-level item. Plan for asteroids – some will be huge, some will be small, but give yourself space to manoeuvre. Until you clean up the first big item completely, there is no point attacking the other big items. Keep things in a hierarchy so you can monitor, discuss and report on the big-picture items. Keeping an eye on other big-picture items ensures that the delivery team members know what's coming up and have an overall view. It also reassures the business stakeholders that the team has not forgotten about all the other things they need, even if they are not broken down into minute detail.

A hierarchical backlog allows different stakeholders to discuss, report on and analyse different levels of information. It allows the team to plan iterative delivery and divide work into small independent items. It allows the business stakeholders to plan and monitor larger business impacts. Instead of micro-managed control, a hierarchical backlog provides visibility and transparency, removing the need to detail all levels of hierarchy at the start.

We often use at least four levels:

- big-picture business objective, for example, grow mobile subscriptions
- smaller-scale business change that might contribute to that big picture, for example, longer user engagement from mobile devices, better conversion from web to mobile, easier migration from competitor systems
- software deliverables that might support those changes, for example, data import from competitor formats, mobile data preview

- smaller deliverable slices that we could ship independently, for example, file access to competitor systems, importing individual data formats, a mobile preview page

We avoid breaking down large items into smaller ones until we need to populate the lower levels with more information. So for example, until we need to start working on a business goal, we would not even try to identify possible business changes that would relate to that. The goal stays in the plan so people know what's coming.

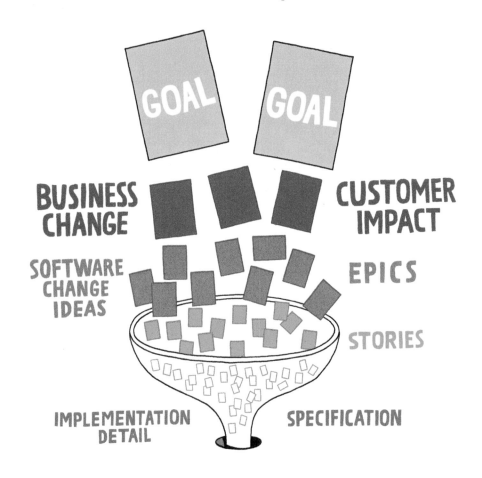

Key benefits

Organising the backlog into several tiers allows teams to reduce significantly the overall number of items, at the same time providing a big-picture view. This means that a delivery team does not need to spend a lot of time managing items, and that nobody has to worry about a lot of sunk cost if the plan needs to change.

A hierarchical plan allows the organisation to react effectively to changing market opportunities. It allows stakeholders to change priorities at any level and quickly discard a whole hierarchy of items if they are no longer applicable. For example, we worked on implementing real-time collaboration for an online document management tool. Half-way through implementation, Google released its Drive Realtime API. This pretty much invalidated the business case for remote document collaboration, as anyone could now build one for free using Google's infrastructure. Because our team had a hierarchy of items, clearly connected to that goal, we could just stop working on anything in that branch of the plan and prioritise a different objective.

A visual connection between different levels also makes it difficult to hide scope creep. Unnecessary features are much easier to spot because there is a higher-level context for each deliverable.

Similarly, a hierarchical plan allows organisations to benefit from insights during delivery. If everyone involved in delivery understands the big picture, they can make better decisions and stop working on items that do not contribute to the big picture, or propose new ideas that will contribute better. For example, one of the milestones for the collaboration product was about growing the number of users significantly. Half-way through working on that, we got a complaint from a university that they couldn't simply activate the application as expected for their 800 students. The university administrators were used to activating the applications through Google's Apps for Education. We haven't even considered that as an important feature. Assuming that there are other organisations with a similar problem, the actual potential to get new users through Apps for Education was huge. We added the new integration to our backlog, prioritised it over everything else and shipped it quickly. We were able to do that easily because the big picture was clear to everyone – the goals on the top of the hierarchy would be better served with a changed plan.

How to make it work

Please don't regard the four-level hierarchy explained earlier as a hard and fast rule; it's just an example. Experiment with the number of levels and the context for each tier until you find something that works for your environment.

Keep the number of items in each tier relatively small – no more than what's immediately needed for further planning and delivery. The actual numbers of course depend on your environment, of course. Teams that need to coordinate external stakeholders, perform customer research or engage people outside the team might need to keep a larger number of items in the pipeline, so that the delivery team always has enough items to work on. Teams whose business stakeholders are immediately available can most likely live with one iteration's worth of items at the lower levels.

One way to implement this idea is to use a visual board with several horizontal swim lanes to represent different tiers. If you use a physical planning board, colour-coding different levels or using different card sizes are good ways to visualise this. Alternatively, you can represent the same information on a customer journey map, a user story map or an impact map.

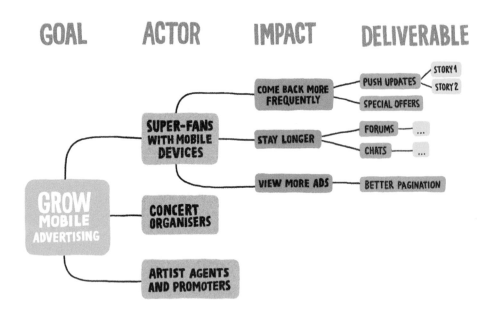

One good way of organising hierarchical backlogs is to use impact maps. An impact map is a visualisation (mind map) of how deliverable scope connects to business goals and the underlying assumptions on four levels. The first level of the mind map is the business goal for a milestone of a project or a product delivery. The second level of the map contains user segments, stakeholders or actors who will be involved in achieving the goal. The third level of the map shows the impacts on users and stakeholders that can contribute to the business goal, or that could hinder achieving the objective. The fourth level of the map is for the deliverables – user stories or even larger deliverables (such as epics) that can cause the impacts.

Impact maps nicely organise the information held in the popular Connextra user story card format ('As a ... in order to... I want...'). Visually, the second level of an impact map corresponds to the persona or role of a user story. The third level corresponds to the value statement, especially when teams use the idea about focusing on behaviour changes. The fourth level corresponds to the deliverable, or the scope statement. This makes impact maps a great tool for grouping and discussing user stories, and moving away from linear plans into hierarchical, adaptive backlogs.

Impact maps have three primary advantages over alternative techniques – they are visual, collaborative, and simple. The simple four-level structure is easy to explain and remember, so the group creating an impact map can focus on sharing knowledge rather than the syntax of boxes or arrows needed to capture information using some other techniques. Visualising the connection between goals and deliverables helps stakeholders to align plans and priorities speedily. One of our clients recently said that two afternoons of impact mapping produced better alignment than weeks of typical planning. The simple format and visual nature of impact maps invites collaboration and alignment, facilitating the work of decision-makers to discover and set common goals for delivery.

Key benefits

Organising a group of stories as an impact map facilitates several levels of decision-making and prioritisation discussions. A map has a single central node, so the stakeholder group first has to pick one big business goal for a delivery. This significantly helps with prioritisation and eliminating unnecessary scope, which speeds up delivery.

Impact maps also facilitate many good product management techniques. For example, because user stories are grouped under related impacts, impact maps provide a way for stakeholders to pick and prioritise on a higher level, as explained in the section Pick impacts instead of prioritising stories.

Because impact maps visually present the information held in the Connextra card format, scope creep is trivially easy to spot. User stories that shouldn't be part of the current release cycle simply won't fit visually into any branches of the impact map.

Impact maps effectively visualise assumptions. When a deliverable is on the map, a stakeholder has an assumption that it may achieve the desired impact on customers. When an impact is on the map, a stakeholder has an assumption that the change in customer behaviour will lead to the overall business objective. This allows teams to design tests to validate or disprove assumptions, supporting better product management. In addition, higher levels of an impact map effectively become acceptance criteria for lower-level elements, helping to reduce unnecessary work. For example, once an impact is achieved, the remaining deliverables in that part of the hierarchy can be discarded from the plan, and the team can move on to delivering the next most important impact.

How to make it work

When you are describing the goal of a milestone – the first level of the map – focus on the problem to be solved, not the solution. Avoid design constraints as much as possible. Creating an iPhone app is not a good goal, improving mobile advertising revenue is.

When you are describing the actors – the second level – think about who can impact the outcome, positively or negatively. There are often three types of actors to consider:
- Primary actors whose needs are fulfilled (for example players with mobile devices)
- Secondary actors who provide services facilitating the fulfilment of the needs of primary actors (such as the fraud prevention team)
- Off-stage actors who have an interest but don't directly benefit or provide the service (for example regulators or senior decision-makers)

To describe the impacts – the third level of the map – think about behaviour changes you are trying to influence. Impacts are not product features. For example better mobile search isn't an impact, but a deliverable. Finding information faster is a good behaviour change to describe instead. Thinking about impacts in this way opens up many options for delivery.

When you get to the fourth level of the map, capture user stories, epics, tasks, product ideas – all the deliverables that could potentially cause a positive impact or prevent a negative one. Then treat them as options, not as commitments.

For some detailed examples and more information on how to create impact maps, see Gojko's book *Impact Mapping*.

The user story map, invented by Jeff Patton, is a popular way of organising hierarchical backlogs. The idea came from the customer journey maps used in interaction design. User story maps connect software deliverables to customer journeys and business workflows, showing how individual stories contribute to the bigger picture and providing a great visual representation of release plans.

A story map is a grid where the horizontal axis represents steps in a high-level user activity, and the vertical axis represents the software delivery schedule (releases or milestones). User stories are grouped in the grid based on the activity or workflow step they contribute to. Stories are spread vertically based on delivery priority, optionally identifying the release they are planned for.

Story maps are a great visualisation tool because they help delivery teams engage business stakeholders in productive discussions about needs, potential solutions and delivery planning all at the same time. A simple tabular structure is easy to understand and feels natural to business stakeholders. Vertical positioning allows

teams to play with different release proposals and explore options before committing to a solution.

Key benefits

User stories are great because they help delivery teams consider the perspective of the users of their software. Story maps take this even further, by putting stories into the perspective of a wider user journey. They help teams get a better insight into why they are building software and how it fits into the big picture.

Apart from a few rare exceptions, any software product is just a part of a wider business activity or customer experience that often starts and ends outside interacting with software. Software might just speed up a certain part of some activity or provide a new way of doing something. Mapping out a user journey helps teams to consider user stories in a wider context, spot missing or unnecessary steps, and create new product ideas.

Organising stories in a tabular way also helps to avoid linear thinking, supporting hierarchical backlogs.

Because of this, story maps help with prioritisation, story splitting and providing focus for release planning. In particular, by mapping out a journey and then considering stories within the context of different actions, story maps help teams think about user stories as options instead of commitments.

Many teams struggle to fit interaction design into iterative delivery. Story maps provide a good framework for considering user interaction journeys and mapping out iterative releases and milestones in that context. It's then much easier to plan work on interaction design, prioritising parts of the journey that are relevant for the upcoming milestone.

By grouping related stories together, stakeholders often see that they can enable certain actions with a simpler choice of deliverables, and postpone more complex stories for later releases. For internal IT initiatives, story maps often open a discussion on skipping some steps or offering a semi-automated solution to get to the initial release sooner.

How to make it work

Create story maps for key user activities – not for software solutions. For example, purchasing a book, booking a venue or attending a concert are good activities to map out. Submitting a rating or posting to a social network site are too low level – they are parts of some higher-level activity and do not deserve their own maps.

As the first step, identify the backbone of the story map – the horizontal axis. Break down activities into high-level steps. The steps should not imply a particular technology or a solution. For example, discovering an interesting book is a step in a purchasing activity that does not imply a solution. Getting book recommendations from a social network is not a key step – instead, it's just one way to discover interesting books. So discovering books would be a good candidate for the key step on the backbone, and social recommendations would be a good candidate story for that vertical. Identifying steps that do not imply solutions will allow you to come up with good ideas later.

Once the backbone is in place, try to identify options for stories. Then move items vertically to plan releases. Think about skipping a particular workflow step altogether or providing a partial solution. For example, think about reducing repetitive work to a single action or providing a manually assisted initial version. This will help identify smaller release candidates that can be shipped sooner.

Create story maps on a large whiteboard or a wall using physical cards or sticky notes, so that you can move them easily. Putting maps into a software tool too early kills conversations. Physical cards allow stakeholders to play with vertical positioning and prioritisation easily and discuss potential iterative releases.

If a user segment has two or three potential journeys involving your system, it's often good to create a combined story map where those journeys are ordered from left to right on the backbone. This will give you a big picture overview and help with high-level prioritisation for milestones. For more complex situations, describing individual journeys with separate maps is better.

If your product has many user segments with potential journeys, consider setting the vision and high-level priorities using an impact map. Each impact is likely to be a change in one user journey, so you can then create a story map for the top priority impact.

For detailed examples and much more information on how to create story maps in practice, see Jeff Patton's book *User Story Mapping*.

CHANGE BEHAVIOURS USING THE CREATE FUNNEL

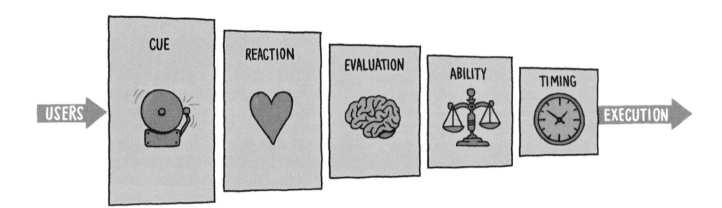

In *Designing for Behavior Change*, Stephen Wendel presents five preconditions for humans to take action:

- Cue: the possibility of action needs to cross the person's mind
- Reaction: the person automatically and intuitively reacts to the idea in a fraction of a second, generating an emotional response
- Evaluation: the person thinks about the action consciously, evaluating the costs and benefits
- Ability: the person evaluates whether the action is feasible given the current context
- Timing: the person judges whether they should act now or later

These five preconditions, along with executing the action, define the CREATE funnel. According to Wendel, all five preconditions need to be met for execution. As in most funnel models, people can drop off from the journey at each stage.

For example, a writing tool might try to help bloggers write more regularly. It could do this by sending custom email alerts to help people set up a routine (cue). Some people will miss the alert completely because they don't read email frequently. The users who notice the alert will react emotionally within a second. Some will ignore the email because they don't feel like writing, and some will spend a few moments thinking about the importance of their writing routine (evaluation). Those who decide that the routine is important will click the link to open a blank page in the writing tool, progressing through the funnel. After a few seconds of staring at the blank page, some people will realise that they don't have the mental energy or inspiration to write (ability), and some will start thinking about the topic of a new blog post. At that point, some people will get distracted or decide to postpone writing because of more urgent tasks (timing). Finally, those who decide that the timing is right will start writing.

This model creates a useful structure for thinking about and creating stories. Great user stories should be focused on causing behaviour changes, and once we have nailed down a particular behaviour change, we can use the CREATE funnel to come up with good story ideas. For example, we could change the cue from email to a calendar alert, which is more likely to be seen. We could create a more positive reaction by changing the visuals or the wording of the reminder. Alternatively, we could provide historical information with the reminder to show how important the routine is, and help with evaluation. We could offer amusing or interesting writing ideas instead of the blank page to help users think more positively about their ability to write. We could also prompt people 30 minutes in advance to finish other tasks, helping to clear their minds for the writing slot (timing).

Key benefits

Just as impact maps and story maps do, the CREATE funnel can help you create a non-linear, hierarchical backlog. Good user stories typically aim to bring about a behaviour change, so you should be able to link a story with a part of the CREATE funnel for the relevant persona. This supports hierarchical planning and prioritisation. Stakeholders can first choose the target persona for the current milestone, then the behaviour they want to influence, and this pretty much helps you nail down one funnel to work on. From there, you can prioritise stories that contribute to that particular funnel.

The model is also useful for splitting stories. If a story is too big and it tries to influence several parts of the funnel, we can split it into several stories that address individual parts. Each small story will still make the overall funnel more effective, so it will still be valuable.

How to make it work

Model the key actions for the target customer segment or persona, and break them down using the different stages of the funnel. You will probably have one funnel for each key action of each key persona. Because the funnel stages imply a progression through time, it makes sense to order the segments horizontally from left to right. Next to each segment, write down the critical features your software provides currently, as the context for further work. Then group stories vertically under each funnel segment, and prioritise by moving more important stories towards the top, and less important stories towards the bottom. Another option for prioritisation is to focus on a single segment first, and try to improve in that area.

Think about establishing some kind of analytical system to measure the drop-off through the funnel, if possible. This will give you a better framework for prioritisation of segments, and a better benchmark for deciding when you can move on to other work.

Once the funnel is visible on a whiteboard or a wall, most teams intuitively create lots of good ideas for user stories that could help improve it. If you get stuck, here are some ideas that Wendel suggests for influencing different parts of the funnel in his book:

- Cue: change cues slightly to reduce the chance of users ignoring them; create associations between user's existing work tasks, routines or habits and the product, avoid concurrent cues that seek actions.
- Reaction: build up trust, improve initial usage experiences.
- Evaluation: help users build habits that will make them skip the evaluation and timing parts of the funnel. Support the user's conscious decision to act, by making tasks easier to accomplish or understand, automating repetition or defaulting actions, remove friction.
- Ability: provide clear guides and action plans, provide small wins, reduce risk of failure.
- Timing: use time-sensitive content, encourage early commitments, align with an event that provides urgency.

Another interesting strategy is to try to invert the funnel, making inaction work for the user's benefit, by shifting the burden of work from the user to the product. For example, after giving consent, the user has no more to do and future actions are automated.

User stories generally bring small iterative enhancements, so they are not particularly well suited for addressing global cross-cutting concerns such as capacity, performance and security. Sure, we can write a user story about improving performance, but performance metrics are probably impacted implicitly by loads of stories. Likewise, certain aspects such as security and usability need to be taken into consideration with every change to a software system, but the requirements don't change that often. Repeating the analysis to surface the same requirements for each user story would be a huge waste of time.

A typical work-around for this disconnect between small iterative changes and global concerns is to just ignore the big picture. When problems surface, a solution is planned as a story. This causes a lot of waste and, of course, waiting for problems to be spotted by users isn't exactly a successful product strategy. Agile processes advocate responding to change over following a plan, but many take this too far and irresponsibly ignore perfectly predictable problems.

The core of the problem is a misalignment of impact: global concerns apply to almost all stories, but the related requirements change on a much slower timescale. A good strategy for dealing with such issues is to have a separate discussion about global concerns once per milestone. This leads to a framework which applies to all work during that phase of delivery, so that the issues do not need to be individually considered for each story.

A way of facilitating such conversations is to create a FURPS+ mind map. (FURPS stands for functionality, usability, reliability, performance, supportability). Draw six branches of a mind map, and label five according to the FURPS acronym. Label the sixth branch with a plus sign. Then let people brainstorm and extend the mind map with their expectations in each area. The sixth (plus) branch is for global items that don't fall into any of the five categories. In *Practices For Scaling Lean and Agile Development*, Larman and Vodde suggest that implementation constraints, resource limitations, interface constraints, operational requirements and licensing requirements all go in this category.

An alternative approach is to create a pyramid of quality based on Maslow's hierarchy of needs, and add an acceptance criterion to each level. The questions that define the pyramid levels (bottom-up) are:

- Does it work? (functionality and deployment)
- Does it work well? (security, performance, capacity)
- Is it usable? (usability, design)
- Is it useful? (behaviour changes, user-level goals)
- Is it successful? (organisational goals)

As an example, here is the set of cross-cutting concerns we set for the second milestone of MindMup:

- People can create and share public mind maps without changes – every change results in a new map (functional)
- Everything is public (security and privacy), and the system works well with maps with less than 100 nodes, on 5 to 6 levels, with up to 1000 concurrent users (capacity and performance)
- User interface needs to be clean but nothing fancy. There can't be any flicker or rough transitions (usability)
- People can quickly knock up a map during a meeting, and share it (user-level goals). We expect at least one external user – not us or anyone we know – to publish a map. We expect at least one external user to come back within one week of creating their first map (behaviour changes).
- The site runs cheaply, costing less than 50 GBP per month. We can baseline user activity to perform marketing tests in future releases (organisational goals).

Key benefits

Key decision-makers can probably participate in a separate discussion on global concerns once per milestone, even if they are too busy to attend every single story discussion. This makes it easier to agree on global targets and make a list of important cross-cutting concerns. These targets then become design constraints that developers always have to consider.

Having a global framework of cross-cutting concerns removes the need to discuss the same things over and over, while ensuring that developers and testers keep the issues in mind while working on each user story. This means that people can prevent problems from ever happening, instead of waiting for users to complain.

How to make it work

Consider creating a checklist of expectations for global concerns such as usability or security. An example security checklist could be:

- No sensitive information (card numbers, passwords) stored unencrypted in database
- No sensitive information printed in logs and audit messages
- No private information (apart from usernames) on non-authenticated pages
- No private information sent using HTTP (only HTTPS)
- Each outgoing communication has a link back to the main website

Many cross-cutting concerns won't fit into checklists because they are not about discrete features. Examples include peak capacity, operational speed and similar sliding-scale aspects. In such cases, try to describe targets as ranges instead of a single value. It's much easier to agree on peak capacity of between 50,000 and 60,000 users instead of a single discrete value.

If you adopt a hierarchical backlog approach, such as impact maps or story maps, hold a separate session to review the global concerns each time a new map is introduced. The business goal and measurements in the centre of the impact map will help you set new targets for performance and capacity, and recognise any need for changes to security or usability policies.

Unlike story discussions, which need to involve the people who will actually implement the story, conversations about global concerns need to involve senior decision-makers. But make sure to involve a mix of senior technical and business people, so you have both perspectives represented. This will help to prevent impractical or impossible targets, but also to challenge people's assumptions.

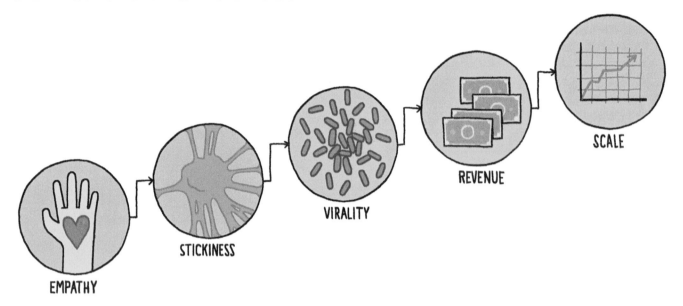

Teams working on new product development often struggle to align stakeholder priorities, jumping between stories aimed to improve short-term revenue, preparing for long-term sustainability (or sometimes world domination) and marketing initiatives that immediately bring new users. All those needs are valid so it's difficult to balance them, especially with a small team and limited delivery capacity. On the one hand, disregarding long-term needs is irresponsible and may prevent sustainable scalability just when the product starts taking off. On the other hand, disregarding short-term needs may cause the product to never take off at all. The problem is actually even worse, because there are different types of short-term needs – user base growth, revenue growth, and the activities performed by a single user or a group of users together.

In *Lean Analytics*, Alistair Croll and Benjamin Yoskovitz suggest a common growth model for successful products:

- Empathy: figuring out how to solve a real problem in a way that people will pay for
- Stickiness: building the right product to keep users around
- Virality: growing the user base organically and artificially
- Revenue: establishing a sustainable, scalable business model with the right margins in a healthy ecosystem
- Scale: growing the business

Obviously the names of the stages are most applicable to consumer software, but similar stages apply to business-to-business software as well. Internal enterprise development doesn't fit well into these stages, because growth and revenue are probably predetermined. However, even with enterprise software it's still worth making sure that the right problem is being solved before preparing for large-scale deployment.

The lean analytics sequence of stages provides an important framework for prioritising user stories. For example, it would be wasteful to focus on virality until customer retention and usage frequency (aspects of stickiness) are good enough. Even if virality improves, lots of users would come but wouldn't stay for long, and they wouldn't come back often enough. It's far better to improve retention and usage frequency first, so that viral expansion has a big impact.

Key benefits

The stages of growth constitute an interesting model for thinking because they can help with alignment and focus. Getting stakeholders to agree on the current stage of growth helps with now/not now prioritisation. Expanding on the idea that great user stories describes behaviour changes, there are only a few important behaviour changes at each stage. For example, most stories in the stickiness stage should be about using the product more frequently, coming back more, using the product for longer periods of time.

The stages of growth are also great as an input for many other product management techniques, such as building a value model and choosing the central goal of an impact map. All these things depend on the context of the current stage.

How to make it work

At each stage, the delivery team should focus on addressing a particular set of risks, by tracking the right measurements and setting concrete objectives. User stories need to follow that focus.

The most important thing to do when using the model is to get all the stakeholders to agree on the stage the product is in currently. When you're just starting out this will be clear, but aligning everyone on the current position might be quite a challenge for work already in progress. In general, trust more the people who argue for the earlier part of the funnel than for the later part. A good way to facilitate alignment is to get data on

current performance for each of the stages and ask key decision-makers if they are satisfied. Choose the first stage that people aren't happy about.

The next step is to choose the objectives for the current stage and identify some quantifiable target metrics which will tell the group that the product is exiting one stage and entering another. For example, define your target user churn, usage frequency and session length for the stickiness stage, and focus on user stories that could create impacts in these areas. Once you have your targets, move on to the next stage and define targets for user base growth. The *Lean Analytics* book has many case studies with metrics from successful companies. You can use these case studies to compare your situation with the market and design checkpoints and target measurements for stages.

Croll and Yoskovitz even suggest choosing *One Metric that Matters* (OMM) at each stage, a representative measurement of progress that will align the entire company and provide a laser-tight focus for product management. The topic of choosing the right metric is far beyond the scope of this short introduction, but the their book has a whole section devoted to it.

The stages of growth model, although temporal, is not supposed to create multiple backlogs. Don't plan too far in advance, and don't collect too many stories for future stages. On the other hand, this model is also not supposed to create hermetically sealed boundaries between stages. It's still OK to make money (and plan stories for doing this) in the stickiness stage, for example. Likewise, it's also OK to prepare for scaling in early stages, or improve virality once you start focusing on revenue. However, the main focus should be on the critical objectives for the current stage. If the majority of your stories are about scaling and the product is in the virality stage, you're prioritising the wrong things.

The MoSCoW model, splitting features into *Must have, Should have, Could have* and *Would like (really Won't do)*, still seems to be the standard way of prioritising work items. One of the biggest problems with this model, which we constantly see working with clients, is that most of the items end up in the *Must have* category. Lots of teams suffer from the *priority one paradox*: the more stakeholders are pressed to identify highest priority items, the more scared they are to leave anything out of that category.

The purpose alignment model, presented by Niel Nickolaisen in *Stand Back And Deliver*, is a good way to avoid that paradox. It is by far the most effective triaging system we've used on software projects. The model requires stakeholders to ask two questions for each item:

- Is it mission critical? (Can the business run without it?)
- Is it market differentiating? (Does it bring customers, provide competitive advantage or something similar?)

Once these questions have been answered, items can end up in one of four categories:

- Differentiating: both mission critical and market differentiating. This is the area where organisations should focus most of their investment. For such items, good just isn't enough, excellence is required.
- Parity: mission critical, but not market differentiating. These are things that have to be done, but they can just be good enough. Making them significantly better than the competition is an over-investment.

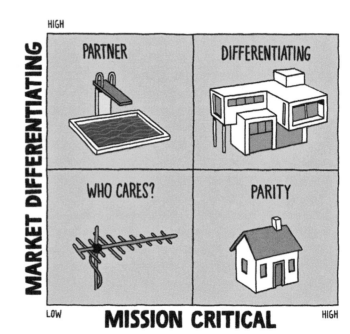

- Partner: market-differentiating opportunities that aren't mission critical, for example opening up an experimental sales channel using mobile devices.
- Who cares: ideas that aren't mission critical or market differentiating.

The purpose alignment model provides useful ideas on how to deal with each category. The entire parity category is a great candidate for off-the-shelf solutions, outsourcing, or just doing the simplest thing that could possibly work. For stories in this category, seriously consider just integrating with something existing instead of building your own software from scratch. Items in the partner category often don't have off-the-shelf solutions, but the organisation doesn't have internal expertise, so it makes sense to partner with someone else who has that knowledge.

Key benefits

Categorising items according to purpose alignment helps organisations refocus efforts. Without using a model such as this one, most of the work is often devoted to creating complex versions of 'must have' items, even if they could in reality just be good enough.

For example, an issue-tracking system for customer support is often mission critical. Without a way to track issues, there would be no real customer service, but for most organisations the issue-tracking component doesn't deliver a competitive edge. Yet far too often organisations build their own issue-tracking system, and waste a huge amount of time and money on maintaining those monstrosities. Unless customer call handling is really what sets the business apart from the competition, it would be much better to change internal processes so that they can work with an off-the-shelf solution or pay a third party to customise an existing system to the just-good-enough level.

We facilitated several workshops where stakeholders decided to simplify their business processes instead of complicating internal IT systems after realising that most of their 'must have' items are actually just parity features.

A major advantage of the purpose alignment model over MoSCoW is that it has two categories for 'must': differentiating and parity. They are both mission critical,

but the former creates value and the latter provides the necessary foundation. It's easy to separate out the items we must invest and excel in from those that just have to be good enough.

How to make it work

The original purpose alignment model talks about business processes, not software features. Since you are working with user stories, the value statement ('In order to...') is most likely to help you do purpose alignment, not the deliverable ('I want...'). If you've inherited a large number of user stories, or business stakeholders insist on detailing things into minute items, it's best first to group stories by business activity or area of impact, and then sort the higher-level items into quadrants of the purpose alignment model.

If a story ends up in the parity or partner category, question whether it really needs to be developed by your team, or if it would be better to integrate with an existing solution or perhaps outsource it so you can focus on differentiating items. If you decide you do have to implement a parity or partner story yourself, make sure you discuss what would make it good enough. This is where the QUPER model could well prove useful. Any stories in the parity category that involve innovative solutions or complex changes need to be challenged immediately.

Remember that items might move from one category to another as the business opportunities change over time. For example, a mobile sales channel might be in the partner category now, but if it takes off and becomes a major source of revenue, then it could move to the differentiating category. In such cases, it's worth revisiting the assumptions and doing some more planning.

Large-scale effects are a potential blind spot for any kind of frequent iterative planning, including user stories. Many teams find themselves in a tight spot by ignoring stakeholders who only function at the big-picture level, such as people involved in corporate politics and external regulators. A good way of preventing nasty big-picture surprises is to complement user personae with some kind of large-scale stakeholder analysis.

User personae are now pretty much mainstream and many good books describe ways of creating good personae and using them for driving user stories, so we won't repeat them here. But these books mostly focus on users who receive value, or people directly involved with the day-to-day service that the software provides. Teams rarely consider people who do not get value or participate in providing a service using software, but have an interest in the initiative or a hidden agenda that might interfere with the plan. Alistair Cockburn calls these stakeholders off-stage actors in *Writing Effective Use Cases*. This is a great name because it immediately conjures up the mental image of someone behind the curtain.

We know of a project at a large UK gambling company, where two years of good work were shelved indefinitely after a new stakeholder suddenly got involved because of a political risk to his corporate fiefdom. To avoid problems such as these, where a new stakeholder suddenly stops a team in its tracks, try creating a stakeholder chart. The stakeholder chart is a simple stakeholder analysis method, described by Dave Gray, Sunni Brown and James Macanufo in *Gamestorming*. It typically takes 30 minutes to an hour, and it should ideally involve the entire team.

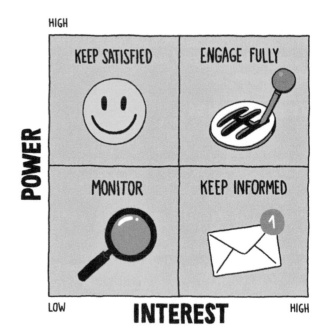

To create a chart, get the group to begin by listing as many stakeholders as possible on post-it notes, especially thinking about any people or groups with an off-stage interest. Gray and colleagues suggest starting with the following questions:

- Who will be impacted by the project?
- Who will be responsible or accountable for the project?
- Who will have decision authority on the project?
- Who can support the project?
- Who can obstruct the project?
- Who has been involved in this type of project in the past?

In the second step, create a 2x2 grid on the wall or a whiteboard, with axes labelled interest and power, and group the post-its according to how important your product or initiative is to a stakeholder (interest) and how much ability they have to bring about their preference about a topic (power). This will tighten your expectations and improve your awareness of how much you need to work with different groups. For example, you might have strong supporters who will work in your favour but don't really wield a lot of organisational influence, and there might also be groups who can stop you at will but don't particularly care about the work unless you mess up. Each of these groups of stakeholders requires different involvement. The first group might be willing to put up with half-finished stories, use manual workarounds and provide frequent feedback. The second group is likely to want finished and polished work, and will not provide many opportunities for feedback and engagement.

Key benefits

A stakeholder chart helps you not to forget big-picture stakeholders who won't necessarily appear in user stories. It is particularly useful when the key to achieving desired outcomes is changing the behaviour of other people, especially in politically charged situations.

The chart creates a shared agreement in the delivery group about how to interact with different types of stakeholders, so you can get the most out of each type.

It can also provide a useful input for story maps or impact maps, helping you to remember additional important actors or personae.

How to make it work

The group of stakeholders is contextual and dependent on the outcome you are trying to create, so make a stakeholder map only once you know the goals of a milestone, and revisit it before starting another milestone. Teams who build a component of an internal software platform normally work with the same group of stakeholders most of the time. Teams who build consumer products often have to significantly change their stakeholder maps between products or even milestones.

Although you can get the information about their scale of interest from the stakeholders directly, the power scale will have to be assessed internally by the team. In politically charged organisations, it would probably be best to identify high-interest/high-power stakeholders first, and then invite them to a workshop to complete the rest of the chart.

In *Beyond Requirements*, Kent McDonald advises different strategies for each stakeholder group:
- Low interest, low power: provide general information and monitor them, to make sure their interest or power does not change during delivery, but do not bore them.
- High interest, low power: keep informed and encourage detailed feedback. Subject-matter experts often fall into this category. Although this group does not have a lot of power, they might involve more influential groups if they feel that their concerns are being ignored or their interests are in danger.
- Low interest, high power: engage infrequently to understand and satisfy large-scale needs. Involve in milestone activities, such as creating or reviewing business goals and impact maps.
- High interest, high power: work closely with these people, engaging them fully and ideally making them part of the delivery group.

For practical information on making this method work, check out the *Gamestorming* book, and also *Everyman's Prince*, by William Coplin and Michael O'Leary, which explains a similar analysis technique called the *Prince Chart*.

NAME YOUR MILESTONES

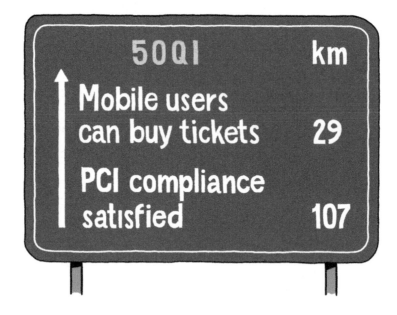

Planning releases based on business deadlines or milestones is an essential part of iterative delivery for teams that are not at the level of product and process maturity to make delivery of individual stories possible. Planning with business milestones is useful even for teams that can deploy individual stories, because most product owners need to track progress against business goals that are typically expressed at a higher level than individual stories. However, teams rarely devote sufficient time to planning their milestones. Milestones often get technical or generic names, such as 'Release 1.1', 'Beta', or 'MVP', which makes it difficult to create effective plans around those milestones.

Identifying stories within business milestones helps connect the work being done at the coalface with the higher-level objectives and governance of the team's stakeholders. To make story selection easier, name milestones with as much care as you would take for naming stories, or even more. Like a story, a milestone represents an increment in business value, and clearly articulating the value that each milestone represents is essential for engaging stakeholders in practical discussions about the details of what belongs inside or outside the scope of each milestone.

Rather than using generic names, it is better to name a milestone according to the capability represented by the set of stories included in it. Name these milestones as *assertions of capability*, for example 'Mobile users can buy concert tickets', or 'PCI compliance satisfied'.

Other styles include the kind of statement you would see on a billboard advertising your new product version, or a bullet point in a key features list on the back of a shrink-wrapped product box.

Key benefits

Choosing good names for business milestones improves stakeholder engagement with the story prioritisation process, and supports planning with hierarchical backlogs. Naming milestones in the early stages of product planning can help to avoid user story hell, as it encourages teams to identify story details for the upcoming milestones, but defer the details of stories in later milestones.

Meaningful milestone names make it easier to track overall progress and communicate priorities and release opportunities to those outside the team. Stakeholders can make sense of overall product evolution and delivery progress according to the named milestones that have been achieved and that are still in progress, without having to go into the details of individual stories.

If stakeholders are concerned about achieving delivery deadlines, they can have meaningful discussions with the product owner and the team about which stories are included in the deadline, and whether it makes sense to move whole stories out of a milestone, or slice them to reduce their size, or identify another valuable milestone with less functionality.

How to make it work

Don't confuse milestones with epics. True epics are simply large stories that satisfy all the other INVEST criteria but are too large to be implemented in a single iteration. However the term is often used (or misused) to represent the whole of a subject area or topic, such as 'reporting' or 'dashboard' or 'personalisation'. While such topics are useful during early product planning as a way of identifying areas of functionality a product may have to include, it can be unhelpful (and plain bad planning)

to assume that an epic must be delivered in its entirety. In any topic there are always more potential features and stories we can come up with, but when all the stories are ordered by priority it is rare to see any single epic reach completion before another one must start.

Milestones, therefore, should describe noteworthy points where a cohesive product increment could be delivered. Typically that means including stories that bring improvements in many different areas, providing a balance of features across your product's end-to-end capabilities. It can also mean including the juiciest slices of several epics, leaving the other slices for later milestones.

Start with a very broad division of stories in a backlog into two groups, such as *day 1 and later*, or *simple version and full version* or even *now and not now. Stakeholders often put more into the first group than* the second, but it is better to do the reverse. Subdivide the first group again, but this time give the new milestone a meaningful name. If there are fewer stories in the first milestone than after it, you are making progress. Continue this process, subdividing whichever group has the most stories in it. Stop when it becomes too hard to give each milestone a good name.

With several named milestones in place, check again what stories are planned for each milestone. Does every story make a meaningful improvement to its milestone? If not, move it. The aim is to have as few stories in each milestone as possible, without creating artificial milestones.

Make this an ongoing process. A story map or product backlog is a living thing that should always reflect the latest plan, based on all the information the product owner has available to them at the time.

Almost always in such situations people first come up with a deliverable ('I want...') and then justify it with a plausible excuse ('In order to...'). They invent a user segment ('As a...') at the end, without a lot of thought. Such stories can be easily spotted because they specify a completely generic user segment ('As a user...') or even a system component ('As an LDAP server...'). Inexperienced teams rarely challenge such stories, and even if they do, the user segments are just changed to arbitrary names. A team we recently worked with had more than 30 different user segments in their medium-term plan. It's nearly impossible to prioritise effectively if a team is trying to satisfy 30 different segments at once, let alone achieve something big.

Working with user personae can help, but it doesn't completely solve the problem. We often meet teams that have defined three or four key personae, stuck their descriptions and pictures on a wall, and have still written a load of stories for other roles.

If you find yourself in this situation, a good trick is to try to limit the number of user segments targeted in a particular milestone. At the start of each milestone, let stakeholders pick target segments first, and then you can drive prioritisation during the milestone based on those choices.

A team we recently worked with was restructuring the sign-up process for their product, allowing users to log on through social media accounts. The stakeholders identified Twitter and Facebook users as important

When business stakeholders aren't experienced with iterative delivery, plans based on user stories often turn into streams of consciousness. Anything goes, stories even get reverse-engineered from feature ideas. A common result is that stakeholders feel that they constantly get small improvements, but the delivery team has no capability of achieving anything big.

segments for this milestone, and agreed that everything else could be postponed. During a discussion about Twitter users logging in directly, the team ended up with acceptance criteria involving several large changes to administrative reports. We challenged the scope, arguing that the reports were not there to help Twitter users but back-office operators, and split the story into two. Because the milestone was about social media users only, it was easy to argue that back-office report changes fell into the 'not now' category. This allowed the team to reduce the scope of the release significantly and push the stories out faster. Stakeholders were then given the option to include stories for back-office operators in the next milestone. But this turned out to be not as important as some other stuff, so the reports actually never got done. Without a pre-selected set of roles, it would not have been easy to argue about postponing the work which at the end turned out to be unnecessary.

Key benefits

Selecting a limited number of target segments for each milestone prevents stakeholders from constantly inventing new user roles. This makes people think twice when writing stories to justify pet features, and results in better, more focused stories.

Forcing people to seriously consider which user segment would benefit from the story, if any, helps to avoid generic stories such as 'As a user' and completely prevents fake stories such as 'As a remote API'.

For teams working with a large number of stories, pre-selecting roles for milestones also helps significantly with prioritisation, and allows stakeholders to make now/not now decisions more easily.

Lastly, a fixed set of roles helps to reduce the scope of stories and earlier delivery of value.

How to make it work

Think small: instead of a larger milestone that addresses the needs of five target user groups, think about five smaller milestones aimed at a single target segment each. Is there a group that could bring more value or reduce risk significantly if they got their stuff first? Give milestones meaningful names to provide focus before choosing target segments.

It's OK for a milestone to include more than one user segment, particularly if they are related. For example, stories dealing with phone customers and customer service operators might be interrelated and both required to deliver a bigger-picture outcome. However, we'd strongly challenge the need for stories involving accountants to be in the same milestone. Don't reject additional user segments outright, discuss and challenge them. For example, in the Twitter log-in situation, if the additional functionality is core and central to the business, it would be stupid to postpone it even though it helps back-office operators. In this particular situation, the reports were in the nice-to-have category and the stakeholders preferred to postpone them. Pre-selected roles were enough to start a good discussion and allow them to make better decisions.

For teams working with a larger number of stories, it's useful to have two sets of stories going into a milestone. One involves stories for chosen user segments, and the other contains all ideas proposed for other segments. All stories involving other user segments are effectively postponed, so stakeholders should know that they won't even be available for prioritisation.

Pre-selecting roles for stories doesn't mean completely ignoring any other urgent work, such as critical bug fixes. See the section Don't push everything into stories for some good ideas on how to deal with such work.

51

DISCUSSING STORIES

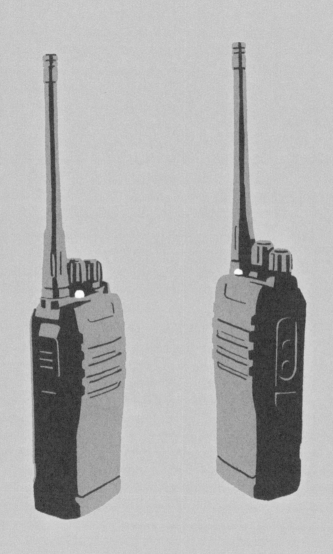

USE LOW-TECH FOR STORY CONVERSATIONS

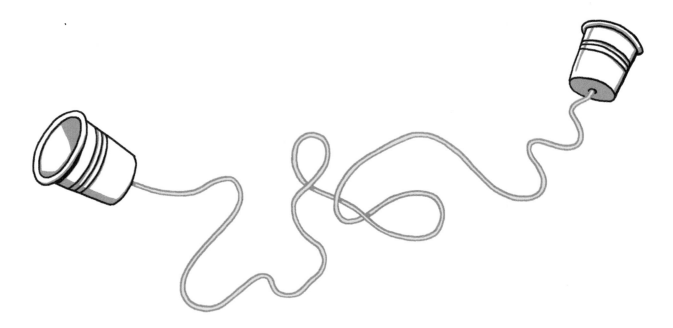

54

Good user stories are a reminder to have a conversation. They are there to facilitate a discussion, not a presentation, not a monologue, and definitely not a session where ten people stare at a projector screen while one person struggles to type.

Communication technology has advanced in giant leaps over the last few decades, but we have yet to see a gizmo that facilitates a discussion as well as a flipchart or a whiteboard. Many teams destroy a conversation by tooling up too soon. They try to record story discussions in Excel or a testing tool immediately, often with a projector. This creates a keyboard bottleneck – only one person can act as a scribe and most of the others relax in their chairs and secretly play Angry Birds on their mobile phones.

Projectors or screen-sharing might be necessary for distributed teams, but if all your team members are located in one place please resist the urge to use hi-tech for your story discussions. Whiteboards will do a much better job.

Key benefits

Not using digital media during a conversation allows teams to focus on the topic at hand, rather than text alignment issues, bold formatting or guessing the right syntax. It's important to record the results of a conversation, but that can be postponed. With fewer distractions, discussions around whiteboards are faster and more productive than discussions around a technical tool.

Another benefit of using a whiteboard is that people can capture their ideas in any way they see fit. Tools typically take away that flexibility, and constrain the discussion to one particular format. If Excel is on the projector, you're pretty much guaranteed to end up with a table even if a list of bullet points would do a better job. A whiteboard allows people to draw pictures, connect boxes with arrows, write sentences, order things into tables or lists, scratch things out and start over easily.

How to make it work

Projectors, spreadsheets and other high-tech gizmos can play useful roles in exploring what a software system does at the moment, or looking at the competition, but shut them down once the real conversation starts. Make people stand up and write. This will lead to a much faster and much more productive discussion.

Use physical index cards and sticky notes instead of collecting information on virtual card walls. Digital card walls are great for tracking and sharing, but horrible for conversations. Physical cards are much easier to create, move, throw away and annotate. Because of that, it is much faster to change priorities on a physical board than inside a digital tool. Digitise the results only after you are happy with the conversation outcome.

If at all possible, avoid meeting rooms with big boardroom tables. They invite people to sit down and negotiate, instead of standing up and discussing. Big tables that block most of the room space prevent people from moving around, so they limit physical interaction. Rooms without tables but with lots of wall space for whiteboards are best for this kind of conversation. Rooms without tables also make it awkward and difficult to use laptops, so people will be more engaged in conversations. With tables, open laptops often distract participants with instant messaging and email.

Digital whiteboards are not yet as effective as a physical ones. The technology might change in the future, but at the moment all digital boards introduce a significant time lag while writing and require people to hold the pen at exactly the right angle, which is just distracting.

If you do not have enough whiteboards, get some whiteboard film (some shops sell this as whiteboard material or Magic Whiteboard). The film sticks to a wall with static electricity so you can put it up and take it down easily. Whiteboard film will give you a larger working surface than a flipchart, and has the added benefit that you can easily take the results with you, unlike a typical whiteboard that stays in the meeting room.

If you absolutely have to discuss stories remotely, aim for visual and communication aids instead of tools which constrain you to a particular way of writing things down. Many teams we worked with had reasonable success using video teleconferencing equipment to record and show the contents of flip charts or whiteboards to remote team members. For situations where team members can form small groups in different locations, getting each group to work around a whiteboard and then taking a photo of the result to share with the entire team during a joint remote video discussion might be quite effective. If most of the team is in one location, a high-resolution video camera pointed at the flip chart to stream the discussion to one or two remote team members works well also.

If that's not an option for you, collaborative document editing is probably the best option. In that case, try to use a tool which allows all participants to type concurrently, instead of having the conversation blocked by one scribe. The best tools are the ones which don't constrain you too much, so people can experiment with different ways of writing things down. Google Docs are an OK option in this case. For discussions involving only two or three people, remote screen-sharing might work well also.

56

Teams working with user stories show progress through demonstrating working software regularly, normally at the end of an iteration. There are different styles of running a demo, with varying degrees of formality and preparation. At one end of the scale (let's call it the *wrong end*) there is no demo at all and no other activity. Close to this is some sort of roll-call of stories or tasks completed, perhaps by reference to a report in a task-tracking tool or a burn-down chart, without any actual demo of working software. Around the middle of the scale is the common practice of having developers or testers in the team do an off-the-cuff walkthrough of each story for the benefit of the product owner, who might be seeing the finished results for the first time. Further along the scale, the demo is based on prepared examples that have been tested before the event.

At the *right* end of the scale, the team regard the demo as an important event, it is open to a wider audience, and senior stakeholders have the time regularly scheduled in

their diaries. The team know it is a high-stakes moment, and therefore the demo is well prepared and rehearsed. The product owner does the demo, already familiar with all the completed stories. They introduce each story by reference to the business value it brings, demonstrate it using well-chosen, compelling and illustrative example scenarios that give the audience quick understanding of what it does, and confidence in the robustness and completeness of the implementation. The demo may also make reference to acceptance criteria for each story.

At this ideal end of the scale, the end-of-iteration demo is a slick production. Whether or not your team actually achieves this nirvana, starting with this goal for each iteration forces a virtuous chain of dependencies that will help the team succeed. It requires a clear idea of what will make each story 'sing', which requires time for the product owner to rehearse a good demo of each story, which requires that the story is completed and thoroughly tested before the end of the iteration.

The quick idea is this: when the team is discussing a story, in the context of understanding the acceptance criteria or exploring key examples, start by asking the question, *'How will we demonstrate this story?'*

This simple act of thinking ahead to a time in the (near) future when the story is complete focuses the minds of all present upon a shared vision of the demo scenarios. This allows the team to pull the required functionality from a common understanding of the end goal.

Key benefits

The demo event is important for many reasons, beyond just the basic agile principle of measuring progress through working software. An end-of-iteration review can be an important morale booster for the team, who can reflect upon their achievements and celebrate their success. It encourages the principle of flow, so team members focus on completing whole stories in priority order rather than having many in progress. The delivery team can stop starting and start finishing. The demo gives stakeholders outside the team a very tangible sense of the real state of the product, and it is an opportunity for them to give valuable feedback to the team.

During planning, thinking ahead to demonstrating the story makes the team focus on what can be achieved in the (inevitably short) period between now and that big moment. This can encourage splitting larger stories in order to focus on the most valuable core. It ensures that the product owner can articulate the business value. It leads to identifying the outputs. It encourages debate about interesting examples versus less interesting ones.

From the product owner's perspective, having a coherent answer to the question 'How will we demonstrate this?' ensures that there is a common understanding of the acceptance criteria for the story, before the team commits to it. It can serve as the draft script for the actual demo, and details can be added or embellished as the story takes shape. It gives a starting point for testers on which to base acceptance test design as well as sparking ideas for exploratory testing.

How to make it work

The ideal demo described earlier does not have to be your starting point. Whatever you are doing now at the end of each iteration, your aim is to nudge your team a little closer to the right end of the scale each time.

The first simple step is to encourage or reinforce your team's commitment to the idea of the demo as the proof of their efforts, the measure of real progress, the moment of truth, the closing ceremony of the iteration. Make a big deal of it. Bring food. Make it feel like the celebration that it should be.

As you get better at demos for the team, invite more external stakeholders to attend. Ask for feedback, invite questions and comments. Mention upcoming stories that they may be interested in seeing at the next demo.

When the team first gets together to discuss a story and answers the question 'How will we demonstrate this story?' make sure you let the testers riff off the answer. That way they will come up with better examples, more interesting details, more discussion-provoking edge cases.

Take the answer seriously, and when it comes to the end of the iteration, demonstrate the story the way you said you would.

DIVERGE AND MERGE

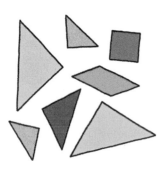   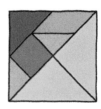

Discussing user stories instead of writing down all the details is a simple idea, but organising an effective discussion is rarely easy. This is especially problematic with larger teams. Without strong facilitation and time management, a discussion of stories can turn into yet another boring meeting.

Groups of 4 to 5 stimulate participation and discussion, but anything larger often encourages one person to hold a sermon and everyone else to check email on their phones. Larger groups often also use projectors and presentations, falling into all the problems explained in the section on using low-tech for story conversations.

Our preferred way of facilitating story discussions for teams of 10 to 20 people is to split the team into several smaller groups, get groups to capture their understanding of a story using examples, then bring the groups together to compare results. Splitting allows different groups to explore their understanding and collect questions faster than with a large team. Groups use concrete examples to show their understanding, so it's easy to compare different outcomes. Bringing groups together helps to coordinate and identify sources of misunderstanding. After several cycles of splitting and bringing groups together, all team members have

a pretty good idea about the contents and the scope of a story. In *Practices For Scaling Lean and Agile*, Craig Larman and Bas Vodde call these cycles diverge and merge.

Key benefits

Diverging and merging helps to engage a large group, and to increase the participation of individual team members. With ten people in a meeting, one person can easily tune out. That's much easier to prevent with a smaller group. In a smaller group each person has to compare their understanding with the rest of the team, so it becomes easier to spot sources of confusion.

Breaking into several groups also prevents a fake consensus. In *The Wisdom Of Crowds* James Surowiecki shows how people with a similar background tend to work towards a consensus, even if the direction is not correct. By diverging and merging we can minimise this effect. Each subgroup works towards a consensus, but different groups can still go in different directions.

The merging part makes it easy to identify potential sources of misunderstanding and differences in opinions by comparing the examples from different groups.

The diverge and merge cycle is also a great example of set-based design, a lean problem-solving technique where several solutions are built in parallel and then combined. Set-based design is more costly but much faster than having just one group work on a problem. Applied to story conversations, this means that the team learns and discovers the right solution faster when diverging and merging than as a single large group. With short iterative delivery cycles, time is often the critical constraint, so faster is better even if more expensive. Individual subgroups tend to explore the story from different perspectives, discovering different questions, knowledge gaps and inconsistencies.

Finally, diverge and merge cycles help to avoid reliance on a single source of all knowledge. It's easy for one person to dominate the discussion with a single large group. This puts a huge responsibility on that individual to be correct all the time and know everything. When the group breaks out for independent discussions, the domination problem does not exist. Everyone has to participate and the team quickly identifies alternative solutions and opportunities.

How to make it work

Get groups to use concrete examples to capture their understanding and write those examples down on a whiteboard or a flipchart. This is imperative because it provides the ammunition for merging discussions. Concrete examples are easy to compare, which means it is easy to identify sources of misunderstanding among different groups. We ask groups to start writing down three to four very simple examples as soon as possible. This helps to set the structure for further examples, but also gets people to write quickly. People often get stuck trying to come up with complex boundary conditions, but they will come naturally once the first few really simple examples are on the board.

To get the best results, communicate that the purpose of the diverge part is not to find all the answers, but to find good questions quickly. Time-box diverge cycles to about 10 to 15 minutes and bring the team together to discuss the results. In particular, focus on the differences among the groups:

- differences in the format or structure of information
- differences in outcomes of similar examples
- things scratched out and question marks

Structural or formatting differences are important because they reflect mental models. If one group considers some attributes important and another group does not, we need to align. Perhaps the first group is going too far, perhaps the second group is not considering important edge cases.

Differences in outcomes of similar examples clearly show potential misunderstandings, so they need to be discussed and ironed out.

Corrections, things scratched out on whiteboards and question marks are a sign that a group had an important discussion and identified things that might not be clear to others as well. These should be discussed with the whole team.

It's often useful to choose a facilitator to keep track of time and lead the discussion during merging. The facilitator is also responsible for comparing the results of different groups. For teams where one person is clearly much more experienced and involved in the business domain than others, that person is probably the best choice for the facilitator. Having the most experienced person stand back and observe allows the whole group to benefit from that person's knowledge. At the same time, the most experienced person can easily spot misunderstandings and prevent groups from going too far in the wrong direction.

INVOLVE ALL ROLES IN THE DISCUSSION

There are many situations where involving an entire team in story discussions isn't practical or useful. For example, it's extremely difficult to facilitate a good conversation with 20 people distributed across different continents. Equally, teams that work on more mature products might not need as much alignment across the whole group as those working on completely new initiatives. Finally, some changes simply don't require the whole group to look at them. If you're just changing a button from blue to yellow, it's unwise to use the time of 20 people discussing the exact shade of yellow.

A common mistake in this situation is to delegate the task of analysing a story to just one person. Instead, create small conversations that involve at least one person representing each of the development, testing and analysis roles. A common name for such conversations, which Gojko used also in *Specification by Example*, is three amigos. Janet Gregory and Lisa Crispin call this idea *The Power Of Three* in *Agile Testing*.

Don't get stuck on the number three, though. We've worked with teams where the database administrator had to be present in all discussions, or where a business domain expert and business analyst were different roles and they both needed to contribute. Four or five amigos is fine, as long as all the relevant roles are represented.

The typical way to run a three-amigo meeting is to start with the analyst or business representative introducing a story and presenting a few initial scenarios of how they would see a story working. Then the developer considers the story in the context of the existing infrastructure and probes for potential functional gaps and inconsistencies. The tester then considers how the story might be tested and applies testing heuristics to identify scenarios that the others have not considered. The discussion continues until everyone is happy that they have enough information to start working and that all major risks have been covered.

Three-amigo conversations are best with a flipchart or a whiteboard, but they can also be very effective around a monitor, or even using screen-sharing remotely. If you organise conversations with a flipchart, one of the three amigos is responsible for writing up the results of the conversation and sharing them with the rest of the team. When three-amigo conversations take place around a monitor or using remote screen-sharing, the participants can directly write up the meeting notes instead of collecting them first on a flipchart and converting to digital form later.

Key benefits

Smaller discussions are often faster and require a lot less facilitation and organisational overhead. People are more engaged in smaller groups, and having all roles represented ensures that all the perspectives get covered.

It's also easier to organise an effective remote three-amigos discussion than a remote full-team discussion. Sharing screens or video-conferencing actually works quite well in such situations. That's why the three-amigo discussion is a particularly effective method for distributed teams.

How to make it work

Make sure to involve people who will actually work on delivering the story. A common mistake teams make is to delegate the three-amigos analysis to whoever has time, so the people who actually end

up delivering the software do not participate in the discussions. This creates problems for knowledge transfer: special cases have to be discussed all over again during iteration planning, and a lot of questions have to be answered again. To avoid this problem, try to divide the work upfront and then involve the people who will actually work on delivering and testing a story in the analysis.

It's important to recognise when the entire team needs to know about some important decision or participate in a discussion. If the three amigos end up discussing a major impact on the current architecture or some globally significant feature change, then it might be worth pausing the smaller discussion and continuing in a larger group with the whole team.

In contexts where most stories require a lot of coordination with business stakeholders or third party teams, it is wise to schedule story discussions about one cycle ahead. For example, shortly after the start of an iteration, do the first-pass analysis on stories for the next iteration. Teams that follow flow-based processes in such situations often create one queue (or planning board column) for the three-amigo discussion and a separate queue for confirming the results of the analysis with external stakeholders.

For teams where one of the roles is a clear bottleneck (for example there is only one business representative), it's useful to plan three-amigo conversations upfront around the availability of that role. For example, each pair of developers and testers gets a one-hour slot with the business representative each Monday. Scheduling such meetings ensures that the busiest person can plan other activities so that there is enough time and availability for collaborative analysis. Teams where there are no clear bottlenecks can be more flexible and organise three-amigo conversations whenever people need more information.

MEASURE ALIGNMENT USING FEEDBACK EXERCISES

Conversation is the most important element of developing software with user stories, but the talking has to stop at some point, and work on implementing the story has to start. Common wisdom is to stop a story discussion when people have no more questions. This can be misleading where developers and testers lack experience of the business domain; they simply won't know what additional questions to ask. Feedback exercises, introduced by Gary Klein in *Sources of Power* can make this process more objective.

A feedback exercise is a very quick and effective way to measure whether a group is ready to move on after discussing a story. Someone (typically a tester) comes up with a difficult boundary condition based on the results of the story conversation. Instead of discussing the condition, everyone individually writes down the expected outcome. Everyone shows their answers at the same time, and if they all wrote down the same thing, that's a pretty good sign of group alignment. If people have different answers, then the group is not yet aligned, and they should discuss the different opinions and try to understand the root cause of the misunderstanding.

During larger workshops facilitators can also look for tricky scenarios which individual groups could not complete or found confusing, and run feedback exercises. This is an excellent way to close a story discussion.

For example, Gojko once worked with a team that was introducing customer accounts into their system. One story asked for users to be allowed access to billable resources as long as they had enough money in their account, otherwise they needed to be sent to the credit card payment page. At the end of a discussion, a tester applied exploratory testing heuristics to the structure of the discussion results – and came up with a boundary condition for the feedback exercise. What if the resource cost £10, and the customers only had £9.99 in the account? Almost everyone wrote down that the customers should be sent to the card payment page, apart from the sales people who wrote that the customers should be allowed to access the resource. The feedback exercise quickly showed that people understood the 'enough money in their account' part of the story differently, and opened up a few interesting questions about profit models and credit limits, leading to a much better solution at the end.

Key benefits

Feedback exercises provide a handy closure mechanism for workshops and story discussions. They are the closest thing we've found to an objective measurement of shared understanding. Instead of workshop facilitators asking if anyone has further questions, feedback exercises can provide a good context for disagreements to surface.

If the entire group agrees on three to four difficult boundary conditions, they have a pretty good alignment on what a user story is supposed to deliver. Otherwise, we know that there is still work to be done.

For smaller teams, where diverging and merging wouldn't be possible, feedback exercises are an excellent way to achieve some of the same benefits. By letting people think in isolation about a problematic situation, and then comparing the results, these exercises help to quickly discover differences in assumptions and understanding.

How to make it work

Feedback exercises are driven by questions, ideally structured around some difficult edge cases. It's very important that while everyone else focuses on the boundary conditions in the exercise, the facilitator focuses on the form of the questions. Exercises should ideally be driven by questions that do not lead people to answers, questions that are as open-ended as possible. For example, asking 'who wins the game?' already presumes that the scenario causes a game to end. A more open-ended question, such as 'what happens next?' might reveal that one person in the room does not think the game is over yet.

Don't just ask one question at the end of a discussion, try out a few different ones.

An easy way to come up with some good feedback exercises is to wait for the structure of scenarios to emerge during a story discussion, and then apply standard testing heuristics to input values. If the inputs are numbers, try negative values, numbers close together, very small or very large numbers. When working with dates, try leap years and dates, end of February, end of year, holidays, or some time-zone combinations that might cause problems. When working with names or addresses, try names that are too long or too short, east-Asian Unicode characters and the like. There are plenty of free test heuristics lists online which should inspire you to create useful edge cases. Elisabeth Hendrickson's *Test Heuristics Cheat Sheet* is a great start, as is her book *Explore It*.

PLAY THE DEVIL'S ADVOCATE

Unexpected circumstances are a fact of life for most software delivery teams. Adaptive planning is a good way to turn those unexpected changes into competitive advantage, because adaptive plans facilitate experimentation and help organisations incorporate learning through delivery into future plans. An interesting aspect of this is that some user stories turn out to be bad ideas.

Think about it this way: if all your user stories are always good ideas, you probably aren't experimenting enough, which means you're not using one of the major benefits of adaptive planning.

Great user stories facilitate a good conversation, and teams that can discredit some stories during an initial discussion get more time for better candidate stories. One good way of discovering bad ideas quickly is playing the devil's advocate – intentionally challenging the perceived need addressed by a user story.

The devil's advocate is not just the name of a bad '90s film, it was also an important role in the canonisation process of the Roman Catholic Church. To ensure that there was a really strong case for canonisation, the church officials would appoint one person to argue against a canonisation candidate, even if that meant taking a position that the advocate did not agree with. This opened up a more thoughtful discussion. Asking someone to play this role during a story conversation is an excellent way to spot bad ideas quickly.

For example, a reader of Gojko's blog recently posted a question about defining the acceptance criteria for the story 'As a user I want to register so that I can log in'. Instead of jumping directly into analysis and trying to nail down the acceptance examples, getting someone to argue against the story opens up a discussion on what people actually want. A user of a website never wants to register. Users will suffer registration if it brings them some benefits, but registering, or even logging in, isn't really high on anyone's list of priorities. In fact, having to remember another username and password combination is something people often really hate.

While building MindMup, we had a similar story. Taking the devil's advocate position, we refined the user need into two: continuing to work on a document easily and controlling access to sensitive information. We then divided this story into two clearer stories, and decided to initially implement only the first one. A clearly defined need led us to an alternative solution. We didn't really need to force people to log in and remember another username and password just to be able to continue working on a document. We used local browser storage to keep the last edited document and automatically opened that the next time a user visited. The solution was simpler, provided a better user experience, and it was faster to implement.

Alternatively, a similar discussion might lead a team to understand that it's not the end-user that wants to log in, but legal or compliance managers who want to protect a system against commercial or regulatory risk. Another possibility is that marketing managers want to force people to open accounts so they can advertise additional products.

Key benefits

A big benefit of this technique is discovering bad ideas earlier, and throwing away or refining stories that would just introduce unnecessary complexity into software.

The second major benefit is opening up a discussion on the perceived need and target user segment, which helps to nail down these aspects of a story before a team jumps into defining a solution.

How to make it work

The big risk with this idea is that the discussion degenerates into personal arguments. Playing the devil's advocate is not about being negative, it's about trying to shake things up intentionally to see if a story is solid or not. Two good ways of preventing personal arguments are:

- Choose one person to play the role to start with, then rotate the role story by story to avoid a single target for negative reactions.
- Get the whole group to come up with ideas about why a story might be false, and take turns to present them.

Discarding a story, or redefining the needs and customer segments, is best done before anyone spends too long analysing a solution for the original story. That's why it's best to play the devil's advocate at the start of a story discussion, or even earlier, when the team collects new story proposals.

Try challenging several aspects of the story:
- Argue that the target user doesn't really have the need (I don't want to log in)
- Argue that the target user segment is wrong (someone else wants end-users to do that)
- Argue that the proposed solution is wrong (delivering the solution will not provide the benefit)

DIVIDE RESPONSIBILITY FOR DEFINING STORIES

technically suboptimal and buggy, with lots of technical debt because of bad design decisions. Delivery teams then have to waste a huge amount of time and money maintaining the overcomplicated solution.

The cause of this problem is a common misconception of the stakeholder role in agile delivery methods. The product owner or XP customer should be responsible for deciding what the team will work on. But deciding isn't the same as defining, and this is where things go wrong! Getting business stakeholders to design solutions wasn't the original intention of user stories – but many teams have fallen into this trap. If this situation sounds familiar, here's an experiment that can help you fix it:

1. Get business stakeholders (sponsors, XP customer, product owners...) to specify only the 'In order to...,' and 'As a ..., ' parts of a user story
2. Get the delivery group (team) to propose several options for 'I want...'
3. Both sides together evaluate the options and the business stakeholders decide which one will be implemented

We've done this experiment with teams that misunderstand stories, where their business users fully specify everything in a task management tool, expecting developers to just code without a discussion. Explicitly limiting the scope of what business users are allowed to specify can force a conversation. People can see the benefits of face-to-face discussions instead of handing information over using a task management tool. Conversation is a lot more difficult to skip when one side can't write the whole story on their own. By making the delivery team come up with a solution, this technique can also help to provide a sense of ownership in the delivery team, and wake up their creative side.

One of the most common mistakes with user stories is to expect business stakeholders to fully define the scope. By doing this, delivery teams are effectively avoiding the responsibility (and the blame) for the ultimate business success of a solution. Although a case can be made for this approach, there is also a huge unwanted side-effect: people who are inexperienced in designing software products – business users – end up having the ultimate responsibility for product design. Unless business users have detailed knowledge of the technical constraints of your product, an insight into current IT trends and capabilities, and a solid understanding of your architectural choices, this is not a good idea. We could write a whole book on why this is a bad idea, but Anthony Ulwick beat us to it – read *What Customers Want*, if you need convincing. The end result is often

Key benefits

The major benefit of this approach is that it forces both sides to have a conversation in order to decide on the actual solution. Delivery team members have to explain several options, and business stakeholders have to evaluate them, so this experiment can shake up teams where user stories normally come fully specified from the business side. The collaboration also puts the responsibility for solution design on the people who are good at designing solutions – the delivery team.

Because business stakeholders are constrained in specifying only the role and the business benefit of a user story, they typically think much harder about the impacts they want to cause instead of the features. That itself is a huge step towards preventing the user story stream of consciousness. The stories move from a generic unspecified value ('in order to improve business', or 'in order to sell more') to something very specific ('in order to monitor inventory 50% faster'). This helps everyone to understand the dimension of the problem, and how much is worth spending on solving it, before you commit to a solution.

The third big benefit of this approach is that it forces both business stakeholders and delivery teams to evaluate several solutions, reinforcing the idea of flexible scope and moving analysis from 'did we understand this correctly?' to 'what's the best possible thing to do?'. Expecting to deal with several options also reinforces the idea that there isn't much point in defining solutions in too much detail upfront.

How to make it work

Communicate clearly upfront that this is an experiment and that you want to run it for a while and then evaluate with everyone (business stakeholders and delivery team). This will make it easier to get buy-in. Running process changes as limited, reversible experiments is an effective way to avoid pushback and power-play politics. (For more on this, read *Switch* by Chip and Dan Heath).

Agree at the start that features are not allowed in the 'In order to...' part – this is an easy way to cheat the experiment. The 'In order to...' part shouldn't say anything about what the software or the product does, only what the users will be able to do differently. An easy way to avoid the problem is to have a rule that it must specify a behaviour change, or enable or prevent a behaviour.

Try to propose at least three options for how the software might provide the value business users expect. Faced with only two options, people often just focus on choosing one of the presented alternatives. With more possibilities, the discussion tends to be focused on the constraints, and pros and cons of different ideas, and often inspires someone to propose a completely new, much better, solution.

Let business stakeholders also propose options in the discussion – but not before. Presenting different options and their constraints provides a better decision-making framework for evaluating ideas, including those that business sponsors have in their heads even before the meeting (and they always do have them). It's absolutely fine to pick an option proposed by the business users, if they still think that's the best solution at the end of the discussion.

The discussion should make everyone quickly understand that there is always more than one solution, and that the first idea is often not the best one. Once people are OK with this, and they see the benefits of collaboratively defining scope, you can relax the rules.

SPLIT BUSINESS AND TECHNICAL DISCUSSIONS

There is a lot of software out there built for software developers, but the vast majority of development work is driven by business stakeholders, who can't read program code. This means that most teams need to discuss user stories with business users. At the same time, user stories often involve technical design changes, and those have to be explored and discussed by the delivery team. Although it might sound logical to discuss both the business and the technical sides of the story at once, in many contexts it's actually a horrible idea. There are two possibilities that can happen if discussions with business users involve implementation details. One is that business users view the story discussion as a waste of time, go away and never come back. The second

option, much worse than the first one, is that the next time business users come prepared with pseudocode implementations.

Technical discussions are important, but shouldn't necessarily happen at the same time as the conversation about the business perspective of a user story. Unless your business users are also programmers, split those two discussions into separate, more focused meetings.

Discuss business needs and divide stories according to value with business users, then let them go and do their day job while the delivery team looks at stories from a technical perspective.

Key benefits

Dividing the technical and business discussions allows teams to shorten the business conversation, and use the time of their business users more efficiently. Staying focused on the business needs during a story discussion prevents business users from getting bored. They won't feel as if the story conversations are a waste of their time, and they will be more engaged in future discussions.

Dividing technical and business discussions also allows teams to consider a whole batch of stories when thinking about design changes. Related stories often impact the same functional areas of the underlying software system, so considering an entire group of stories at once often leads to shorter technical discussions and better design decisions. A focused discussion also prevents teams from jumping into implementation details too soon, and instead makes them spend more time on really understanding what needs to be done.

Jumping into implementing something that is not actually needed is a sure way to waste a lot of precious time. Given that user stories are at best rough ideas before the actual discussion, it's not uncommon for delivery teams to propose better, faster or cheaper solutions once they understand what business users are trying to achieve.

How to make it work

If you're working with a team that often jumps into technical discussions with business users, try to agree upfront with the entire team when the implementation details should be discussed. For example, have a separate technical meeting immediately after the user story refinement sessions. Having a clear upfront agreement relieves the pressure to discuss technical concerns while agreeing on the business perspective of a story.

If your team has a formal checklist for preparing stories for implementation, think about adding a separate item about technical design reviews to the checklist. That's often a good way to get into the routine of splitting collaborative requirements analysis from collaborative design sessions. Similarly, if your team is using a visual task board, think about splitting the analysis column into two separate columns for business and technical design reviews.

If some technical implementation has a significant impact on your capability to deliver something, such as a subset of features with not-so-good performance which could be improved later, by all means talk about it and offer options. Choosing between the options is a business decision and stakeholders need to understand possible benefits and trade-offs. But watch out for technical discussions that do not really help in deciding what should be done.

This doesn't mean discussing only aspects of your software directly visible to users. The key question isn't how far something is from a real user, but should the business users care about it or not.

This applies to the user interface, but also components without an interface. For example, building an API to consolidate access to multiple data sources might seem purely technical but the situation is likely to be more complex than that. Matching and unifying records, handling discrepancies, cleaning up data and resolving conflicts should probably be discussed with business users to ensure their needs are met. Database schemas, transaction management, synchronous or asynchronous parsing, handling multiple updates, ghost data and so on are probably best left out of the discussion.

Most good stories are multi-layered. They influence one thing which leads to another which improves some high-level aspect of someone's work. Such stories are very difficult to capture with just a single value statement, and forcing them into any kind of standard story format actually prevents fruitful discussion.

For example, think about an online text editor that enables users to share documents with their colleagues. The first version supports viewing shared documents using the most popular desktop browsers, and the business users are now proposing to extend sharing support to less popular browsers, mobile devices, and older versions of desktop browsers. This change would have immediate direct value to recipients of shared documents, because they would be able to view content on the go, as well as in older and more obscure browser versions. It would provide value indirectly to users who send shared documents, because they would be more confident that the recipients would view the content correctly. This would in turn provide value to the text editor website operators, through deeper user engagement. Better engagement leads to increased revenue from selling premium features. Better sharing compatibility also improves built-in viral marketing, because people who receive shared documents might sign up and become users, at first using free features and paying for premium features later. This story has at least four levels of value. Selecting any single level and focusing only on it doesn't really paint the right picture.

- 'In order to *increase revenue*, as a *site operator*, I want better browser compatibility for shared documents' sounds too high level and disconnected from reality, in particular because users do not pay for sharing or viewing.
- 'In order to *increase viral sign-ups*, as a *site operator*, I want better browser compatibility for shared documents' sounds more down to earth but doesn't really capture the core reason behind the change.
- 'In order to *increase user engagement*, as a *site operator*, I want better browser compatibility for shared documents' describes the core reason behind the change, but it's not clear why the deliverable would lead to the value.

- 'In order to *view documents in mobile browsers more easily*, as an *anonymous recipient of a shared document*, I want better sharing compatibility' sounds as if the user group is completely irrelevant for the bigger picture.
- 'In order for *recipients to view documents easier*, as a *document creator*, I want better browser compatibility for shared documents' sounds as if it's a nice feature to have but not contributing to the bottom line.

In cases like this, we've seen people spend half an hour arguing which of the values and users to put into their prescribed story format, only for the business users to get up and leave, insisting that that they don't care about what's in the story, but it has to be done, and done yesterday. At that point, the story turns into an all-or-nothing task, and it becomes incredibly difficult to slice it, negotiate scope, or prioritise iterative deliveries.

To get the most out of stories, think about several levels of value, and try to identify through discussion whether there is a story within a story. If you end up arguing about which value statement to choose, just list several of them and capture the whole chain of reasoning. Then invest the time you saved into the actual discussion about the story, instead of wasting it on wording.

Adrian Howard had a great example of this: a story that allowed users to sign up through social networks. The original story proposal was:

As an unregistered user I would like to sign up using Twitter so that I don't have to re-enter all of my info and remember a new password.

Investigating further levels of value, they discovered that this could bring the following benefits to the organisation:

- decreased drop-out during registration
- having access to people's social network accounts for marketing purposes
- opening a path for further social network integration features

In the original story description, potential business value was masked in trying to meet a perceived user need, and the story did not explain the big picture directly. Discussing the three higher-level options further, they decided to focus on decreased drop-out. This lead to a hypothesis that giving users the option to register through Twitter would improve the conversion rates by 5%. This led to a quick test – a link to register via Twitter which just measured clicks and displayed a message that the feature would be available soon. After disappointing click results, they decided to drop the story and build something else instead.

Key benefits

When the whole chain of reasoning is clear, it's much easier to have a useful discussion on what the story really needs to deliver and to design experiments to validate the underlying assumptions.

How to make it work

For a start, think about the two most typical levels: the value to the user and the value to the organisation selling or operating the software. If you can find a story that brings both, then you have a win-win situation. Thinking about these two levels often opens up a good discussion about user needs or a whole chain of events in between keeping users happy and increasing or protecting revenue. Then try to focus on the higher-level values first, and prove that they actually make sense.

DISCUSS SLIDING-SCALE MEASUREMENTS WITH QUPER

Many aspects of software systems aren't related to the presence or absence of a particular feature, but to a combination of features that together provide value on a sliding scale. Examples of such aspects are performance, capacity, start-up times, operational response times and so on. (These are commonly grouped under the label *non-functional*, which we really dislike because they imply quite a lot of functionality.)

Such aspects are often challenging for teams to nail down because of their continuous nature – they can't be described easily by a single number. Even when the business sponsors come up with something precise, for example 50,000 concurrent users on the website, the numbers sound arbitrary and do not really describe a hard criterion. Why 50,000 and not 45,000 or 55,000? In reality, a story involving such numbers is rarely rejected if only 49,999 users are supported. At the same time, any such criteria also carry a lot of hidden assumptions. Although someone might commit to 50,000 now, they won't expect that a major system rewrite will be required to get to 50,001 tomorrow.

For cases such as these, where value is delivered on a sliding scale, the QUPER model is an excellent way to facilitate discussions. The QUPER (QUality PERformance) model visualises and exposes two types of information about the market need and the proposed architectural solutions: breakpoints and barriers.

Breakpoints are thresholds of usefulness for a particular aspect of a system. The model requires stakeholders to identify three particular breakpoints:

- The *utility* breakpoint is the point where a product moves from useless to usable.
- *Differentiation* is where an aspect of the product becomes a competitive advantage.
- *Saturation* is a point after which any improvements are an overkill, and make no real difference to users.

Breakpoints are interesting because they do not depend on the actual solution, but on the market. They are determined by the expected user needs and the competition.

The other type of information used in the model is related to the proposed solution. QUPER assumes that for most sliding-scale values, the relationship of cost to benefit of potential architectural solutions is similar to an S-curve. There is an initial investment required to get any value (startup costs), then the benefits scale with low investment, but beyond some point the chosen solution no longer applies, and a large investment is required to get more value – either a rewrite or a major change to the architecture. For example, starting from a point where a website does not support card payments at all, there is a significant cost involved in supporting even one transaction: setting up the payment gateways, setting up background queues for payments, implementing payment options and so on. But once that is done, a single payment gateway can probably handle dozens, if not hundreds of payments concurrently. Small investments might be needed to optimise work, but nothing major. At some point, one payment gateway won't be enough. To increase the capacity, there will have to be a significant investment in re-engineering to support multiple concurrent payment gateways, to set up load-balancing among gateways, to install new machines and so on. The points where cost-to-benefit ratio changes sharply are called barriers, and they are related to particular potential architectural solutions.

By visualising breakpoints and barriers, we can expose assumptions and have a meaningful discussion about where our solution is compared to the market and where we want it to be. We can use breakpoints to start a discussion on which area of the model the solution needs to fit into, and define targets for different stories, releases or even phases of a project.

Key benefits

The QUPER model helps to start discussions on sliding-scale requirements because breakpoints are impartial. They do not depend on the delivery organisation or business stakeholders, but on the market and the competition. Discussing numbers that don't depend on anyone in the room helps to avoid subjective opinions and align expectations from the start.

By clearly listing cost options and discussing future changes, the QUPER model also helps to bring out hidden assumptions about future growth. This helps delivery teams and business stakeholders choose the right investment in architecture so future targets can be easily met by iterative delivery, without requiring major rewrites. The discussion helps to avoid over-engineering of aspects that need to be just good enough.

How to make it work

Choose ranges instead of discrete numbers. For example, instead of asking people to agree that a card transaction needs to complete in 3.14 seconds, try to get an agreement that most transactions need to complete in between 2 and 5 seconds. Choosing intervals is much easier because it allows you to group different opinions, and also avoid false failures. The person asking for exactly 3.14 seconds will most likely be happy even if the transaction completes in 3.30 seconds.

When you are choosing an interval, start with the worst-case scenario. People can often agree more easily on a failure condition than on success. For example, it's much easier to get people to think about how many users a website has to support in order for it not to be a commercial failure, than to get everyone to agree on blue-sky thinking about how many millions of customers they will have if the business takes off. Once you have the lower end of the interval, you can present options for iterative delivery, similar to the approach described in the section on splitting stories by capacity.

For best results, mix this approach with the purpose alignment model to identify which part of the QUPER diagram the interval should fall into.

For more information, check out the list of resources at quper.org.

SPLITTING STORIES

START WITH THE OUTPUTS

A major rewrite of a legacy system is arguably the most difficult situation for slicing deliverables into small valuable pieces with user stories. Big legacy rewrites are often a solution of last resort when so many problems have built up that to go on maintaining and adding to the old system is no longer viable. Such projects often have many ambitious goals, such as to speed up future delivery, unlock critical business opportunities, adopt a different architecture that allows for growth and reduce costs by consolidating components. People often see it as a job for a broadsword, not for a scalpel.

But the problem, always, is that the world does not stop for us. While the system rewrite is underway, market opportunities change. It's difficult for business sponsors to resist extending their legacy systems with new features to cater for short-term needs. The target keeps moving, and we've seen too many teams get stuck in a game of catch-up, where unexpected complexities in their legacy system cause delays and the new solution takes far longer than expected to be completed. They end up operating two systems side by side for a long period of time, effectively moving to the new system incrementally instead of by flipping a switch. Sometimes the rewrite just never catches up, and receives a mercy bullet when someone senior adds up the costs.

The big risk for any incremental rewrite is that it never delivers enough functionality for people to start relying on it instead of on the old system. This is why the mercy bullet arrives at the end. Most incremental rewrites fail for reasons that have a lot more to do with psychology than technology. Because it's easier to think about time

linearly, rewrite plans start with the inputs into the system – user interaction to let people register, define metadata, enter some transactional information and so on. These things are sliced into small independent deliverables (via user stories), which are presented to proxy product owners who nod their heads at iteration reviews, but the releases never get to the live system because the end-users just don't care. It's not unusual for the new system to become really useful to anyone in a production environment only after a few months of delivery.

Chris Matts popularised the idea that the value of an IT system is mostly in the outputs it produces, and that the inputs are just means to an end. Instead of thinking about workflows linearly, think about the outputs first. Instead of thinking about the log-in screen, think about the reports. Instead of slicing the future system by inputs, slice it by outputs, and then build up the capability to produce these outputs incrementally.

One of our clients started a huge legacy rewrite project that would see them divide teams differently, use a new programming language, install a new network data grid, consolidate several databases and centralise exception detection and processing by replacing a dozen smaller systems around the world, each with their own set of rules. The outputs were exception reports, and the new system would deliver them better, faster, cheaper and nicer. The team took one exception report that was bad, slow, and ugly, and looked for ways of producing something close to the target, while using the old system as much as possible. The current reports had too much data in them and, though it was necessary to have details for further investigation, it was difficult to see a big picture. So the first slice was to provide a new output, the big picture. The first user story was to produce summary reports with links to old reports for detailed investigation. The team sliced the story further by choosing only one type of activity to report on – the most time-consuming one for exception handling. Then they sliced it further by eliminating custom time periods: the first version would always report on the last seven days. They sliced again by eliminating authentication – although security was generally important, the new summary was not too sensitive, and the sensitive trade details were still protected by the old system in linked reports. The team sliced the story yet further by eliminating on-demand reporting – they would automatically generate the new report every morning and distribute it by email. After twenty minutes of discussion, the solution was no longer broad-sword butchery, but a scalpel operation. The delivery team had something they could reasonably deliver in less than a week, and the business users would get something instantly useful and valuable in the new system. It required talking to only two out of twenty databases, and did not need the new data grid. This plan opened the path for making the first report more flexible (and valuable) incrementally, and provided a nice template for moving all the other reports over incrementally.

Key Benefits

The key benefit of thinking about outputs first is that it becomes much easier to create a sensible incremental delivery plan. Outputs are much easier to slice than inputs because they enable users to achieve something concrete, and people can have fruitful discussions on them. It is more difficult to get a positive answer to 'Can we let people register without entering an address?' than to 'Is an exception report that shows only a country of registration and not the street name and number useful?'. And even if registration without an address is approved, the change is unlikely to reach production and real users. A half-complete exception report that flags serious business issues early will quickly be embraced even if it's not the most secure.

Delivering a valuable output quickly also prevents the mercy bullet approach later on – a system that serves valuable data in production is not as easy to kill as a system that after six months of build-up has great registration forms but does not provide useful outputs.

How to make it work

This strategy is especially successful if there is some critical output that the legacy system cannot produce neatly – aim to deliver this first. People who would benefit from the output are more likely to turn a blind eye on performance problems, an incomplete user interface or temporary workflow issues.

Another key challenge is identifying the right people to involve in the slicing discussion. Proxy product owners in large organisations are conduits of information, but are often not empowered to make decisions. Try to find the people who benefit from an output, who use it for something in their work. They can make better decisions on the scale, completeness and performance, and how to achieve them gradually.

The walking skeleton has long been our favourite approach for starting a major project or a legacy transition. Alistair Cockburn provides a canonical definition of this approach in *Crystal Clear*:

A Walking Skeleton is a tiny implementation of the system that performs a small end-to-end function. It need not use the final architecture, but it should link together the main architectural components. The architecture and the functionality can then evolve in parallel.

Building on this, Dan North formulated the idea of the dancing skeleton. A dancing skeleton not only delivers a small function on the target architecture, it also involves an interface for developers to interact with the environment and experiment. When the users

need a more complex function, developers can make the skeleton implementation 'dance'.

The walking skeleton sets up the main architectural components, and the dancing skeleton approach allows experimentation on the target architecture. Both approaches allow teams to ship something quickly, and build on it iteratively.

Modern technology and delivery approaches, in particular the push towards continuous delivery, enable us to take those approaches even further. We can deliver value with an even thinner slice than the basic walking skeleton and build the architecture through iterative delivery later. We can start with a piece that users can interact with, avoid linking together the architectural components, but instead use a simpler and easier back end. We can then iteratively connect the user interface to the target platform. In the skeleton lingo, don't worry about making the skeleton walk, put it on crutches and ship it out. While users are working with it, build up the muscles and then take away the crutches.

The core idea of the skeleton on crutches is to ship out the user interface early, and plan for iterative deployments of everything below the user interface. The user interaction may change very little, or not at all, while the team improves the back end through continuous delivery. With a good deployment pipeline, back ends can be updated and reconfigured without even interrupting user flow. For example, with MindMup we use multi-versioning when we create scripts and APIs, so we can deploy a new version of back-end functionality without interrupting any active sessions. Users with open sessions continue to use the old functionality until they refresh the page, and they can benefit from updated features on their next visit.

Here are some recent examples of skeletons on crutches in the projects we've been involved in:

* A customer report built with Google Analytics events instead of being hooked into a complex back-end database. It wasn't as comprehensive or accurate as the final thing, but the first version was done in two hours, while the final version took several weeks to implement because of third-party dependencies.
* A document uploader which saved directly from users' browsers to Amazon S3 file storage, instead of uploading to the customer database. The skeleton was not as secure or flexible as the final solution, and did not allow fast searching, but was done in a hour.
* A registration system executed using JotForm, an online forms and workflow system which can take payments. This allowed us to start registering users and charging for access without even having a database.

All these solutions were not nearly as good as the final versions, but they were in production very quickly and allowed users to start getting some value early. Some remained in action for a long time, for example we kept registration through JotForm in production for three months, because it was good enough and there were more important things to do.

Key benefits

A major benefit of skeletons on crutches is early delivery of value. A user segment starts getting some value almost instantly. None of the examples mentioned earlier were particularly difficult to build, but users got value in hours instead of weeks.

Early validation is an important consequence of early delivery of value. Instead of showing something basic to users and asking them to imagine the final fantastic offering, a skeleton on crutches allows them to actually use something in real work. This allows product managers to get invaluable feedback on features and product ideas early and build that learning into the plans for later versions.

For example, the JotForm registration skeleton allowed us to start charging for access months before the overall solution was ready, and the fact that users did pay provided huge validation and encouragement that we were going in the right direction. We were also able to discover some surprising things people would pay for, and change the focus of our business plans.

How to make it work

Aim to deliver the user interface part first, on a very simple architecture. Try to skip all back-end components that would slow down delivery, even if for half a day. Deliver a user interface part that looks and works as much like the final version as possible, to avoid future surprises. Iterate on the interface until you confirm that you're delivering value. Then replace the back end with as few changes to the user interface part as possible to avoid surprises. If you must change the user interface, consider multi-versioning to support uninterrupted usage. Build up capacity, performance, and extend functionality by replacing invisible parts with bits of your target architecture iteratively.

If security or corporate policy needs prevent you from using remote crutches, then consider using simple components onsite. One of our clients was a team in a bank whose corporate procedures required weeks of bureaucracy to deploy an application with access to a production database. The team set up a web reporting application which executed reports on plain text files, retrieved by another application, using Unix command-line tools behind the scenes. This allowed them to deploy quickly, but only worked for quite a limited data set. While the users were happily using the reports in the first few weeks, the team obtained access to the production database and replaced the back end without the users noticing anything.

NARROW DOWN
THE CUSTOMER SEGMENT

At the beginning of a new project, especially a legacy rewrite, teams often claim that a whole underlying infrastructure has to be in place in order to provide any value. The first few releases are announced to be mostly about building up some perceived basic functionality, often with a huge chunk in the must-have category. In these situations it is particularly difficult to slice the work into small and valuable chunks, because the discussion on what is a must and what is optional often leads to a dead end. One good trick in such situations is to avoid the discussion on splitting the deliverables, and instead try to narrow down the target customer segment. Don't give everyone 2% of what they need, instead give 2% of users everything they need.

A good example of this is a back-office application at a bank we worked with. The initial story about capturing trade messages was too big, and a lot of the complexity was around different tax systems. We investigated narrowing down the customer segment as a potential way of slicing the story, and discovered that two people in the department dealt with UK trades, and that the UK does not charge tax on the target transactions. By narrowing the customer segment down from the entire department to just those two people, we had a chunk of work that we could implement in two weeks. It would bring some value quickly, and would be a useful step towards the overall solution.

Another good example is the segmentation we created at the start of MindMup. Right from the start, our key target user persona was a tech-savvy professional who uses mind maps for planning and needs to knock up a map quickly during a meeting. Frictionless idea capture and easy sharing were critical for this, but implementing a reasonably powerful interface with all the sharing needs was a few months of work. By narrowing down the customer segment to people working on open-source or public projects initially, we could disregard security. Such information would be public anyway, so we did not have to authenticate viewers or provide any kind of content control. We could also pass on the responsibility for sharing to the users, instead of building it ourselves. Each map, when saved, would become read-only and get a unique URL that people could send easily by email. Anyone with the URL would be able to view but not modify the maps. Any changes would be saved to a new file, and a new URL. As a result, MindMup went live roughly two weeks after we started building it, and enabled a small segment of users to perform almost everything they needed. In the months that followed, we expanded the feature set for open-source planners, and slowly added security, content controls and sharing for the original target persona.

Key benefits

The biggest benefit of this approach is that a subset of users starts to use the new software quickly. This often isn't the core of the target market, or even the most important group of stakeholders, but someone starts using the new software quickly, which provides invaluable real-world feedback for further development and puts the foot through the door for the new delivery

effort. As soon as real users are benefiting from the new software things become a lot clearer, future planning becomes easier and business stakeholders learn whether their product ideas are working out in the real world.

Depending on the importance or value of the chosen narrow segment, this approach can also help a small group of people solve a problem quickly. That can provide justification for further investment, win political points for internal projects or provide a solid base for A/B testing for consumer products.

How to make it work

Customer segments can be narrowed down by many dimensions. For consumer products, the typical dimensions to consider are territory, age, technical proficiency, location (home, work or mobile), language, occupation, needs and so on. For internal IT or enterprise systems, interesting segments can be type of work, department, their target market (for example selling to small companies or to large multinationals) and so on. Consider multiple dimensions and find one which allows you to deliver just a small subset of functionality and help the targeted users get the information they need or achieve a work objective.

Another thing to consider is that the narrow slice of the target segment does not need to be the most important one. Aim for a segment whose members do not care about a huge part of the target feature set. If you can make a big business impact by selecting a critical subgroup, even better. However any narrow customer segment that allows you to put something useful in front of real users quickly will provide the benefit of fast realistic feedback, and a path to build things up incrementally to increase your segment coverage. In fact, if the delivery of the new system introduces significant business risk, choosing a less important segment to experiment on might make a lot of business sense.

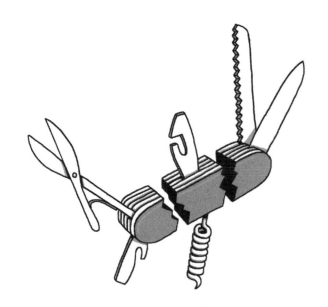

A particularly challenging situation for story splitting is where there is a large technical job to do – for example replacing one database with another, or implementing a major internal redesign. Teams often divide the work technically and then look for chunks which still have value, but a technical split often leads to slices that are too thin to go to production independently, or those monstrosities sometimes known as technical stories.

Any useful way of splitting stories has to break down the technical complexity somehow so that it can be delivered iteratively. But attacking that complexity directly often isn't the most effective way of story splitting. Instead of slicing technical deliverables and then looking for useful chunks of value, try to start from the opposite direction: slice value and look for useful technical chunks.

One useful way of doing this is to ask for a few examples of how the intended deliverable would be useful, and then select those that depend only on a small piece of the overall solution. Extract each of these examples into a separate user story.

Here is a concrete example. We initially launched MindMup using HTML5 Canvas as a visualisation technology, which in retrospect was a mistake. The Canvas standard was at the time still under active development, so new browser versions often introduced breaking changes. Between Google Chrome browser releases 26 and 34, four versions of Canvas came out with changes that broke the graphics library we used. Though we quickly provided explanations and workarounds such as temporarily turning off hardware acceleration, the maintenance cost was unsustainable.

We chose to move the visualisation to Scalable Vector Graphics (SVG), an older technology that was not much affected by new versions of browsers. At first, moving from Canvas to SVG looked like one of those typical all-or-nothing migrations. We knew the solution, but it was just too much work and too much risk to ship in one chunk. It is possible to mix and match these technologies on the same web page, so we could have moved features to SVG incrementally. But the goal here was that the new solution would significantly reduce maintenance costs, enabling us to focus on building up the system instead of catching up with browser development. This is why there would have been no value until the very end – when Canvas was turned off. In fact, mixing both technologies on the same page during migration would significantly complicate things and increase our maintenance costs. To make matters worse, we had spent a lot of time tweaking and improving Canvas performance to handle huge maps, so we knew that there was no way to tune SVG to the same level quickly.

We investigated examples of usefulness as a way of slicing this monolith, and that opened up a way to iteratively ship the changes. One example where SVG would be useful was to stop breaking websites that embedded our maps. When existing users encountered a problem with a new browser version, they would either look at our documentation pages for a workaround, or complain directly to us, in which case we could help them. But there was no easy way of helping anonymous visitors to sites with embedded maps. By migrating to a more stable technology, our users could have more confidence that their visitors wouldn't be surprised. This particular example was an interesting slice which could be achieved quickly. Embedded maps are read-only, so the layout could be calculated by the current system, and we did not have to worry about browser interactions. Users could still create maps using the old technology, but when maps were embedded we could just swap over to SVG. This was our first user story.

The next example of usefulness was improving the initial visit experience. During their first visit to our site, new users would mostly work on smaller maps and use basic functions. To support this, we could significantly reduce complexity and focus on basic interactions and just make sure that maps up to a hundred nodes worked reasonably well. We published this as an opt-in feature, so that users who needed more performance or advanced features could still use the old system.

The next example of how SVG would be useful was that it could benefit from native browser styling capabilities. SVG objects can be styled using Cascading Style Sheets (CSS), a well-known web standard, unlike Canvas where we had to program look and feel. Canvas didn't allow users to style maps easily, so that feature wasn't in the old system at all. However, it was now low-hanging fruit, and it would entice users to opt in and turn on the new drawing engine, providing valuable feedback and de-risking the rest of the migration for us. So the third user story was enabling users to customise the visual style for their maps.

After that, we tackled collaboration, larger maps, mobile users, then more complex interaction such as image drag-and-drop. Each of these areas was driven by some nice examples of usefulness. Instead of building features up until all users could be switched over, we enabled a subgroup of our users to get part of the value with each story, and provided incentives for opting in.

Key benefits

Dividing by value and then looking for useful technical chunks helps to avoid the technical trap of a big risky migration at the end. This approach turns deliverables into a stream of small changes, each valuable enough so that it can go to production and be used by someone. This leads to small, low-risk releases, with each release providing real-world feedback.

Even more importantly, slicing stories by examples of usefulness provides value much sooner to a subgroup of users. People do not have to wait for months until the whole job is done to benefit from specific changes.

How to make it work

List a bunch of options for how the final technical change would be useful, and don't worry too much if they overlap. Among these examples, look for ones where technical delivery would be significantly reduced, where you could reuse large parts of the old system or where you would only need to provide part of the business workflow. For example, tackling only embedding allowed us to remove all interactivity, reuse existing calculations and not worry about performance.

If the larger piece of work is very risky, try to find the first few examples of usefulness that are not really on the critical business path. For example, embedded maps were used by a very small percentage of our overall users, but enough that they could provide useful technical feedback.

SPLIT BY CAPACITY

FIFTY QUICK IDEAS
TO IMPROVE YOUR USER STORIES

84

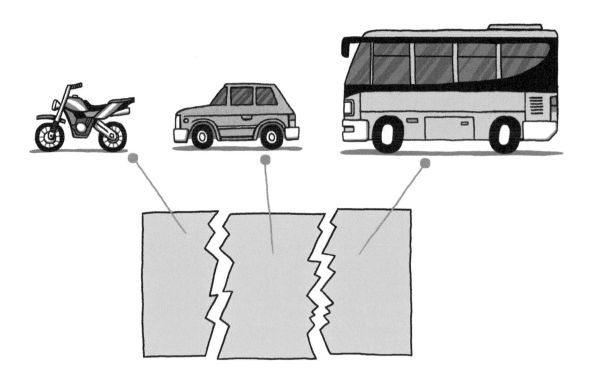

An initial launch of a product or service is often a major hurdle for iterative delivery. Teams often spend months getting all the pieces in place so that they can release a system that actually provides useful functions, and then switch over to more frequent releases. A common justification for this approach is that so many components are necessary for even the first user to start getting benefits that it wouldn't make sense to slice the product into smaller releases. Narrowing down user segments is often a good starting point for changing from a big batch first release to a sequence of small targeted deployments. If that doesn't help, it is often useful to try slicing the plan to progressively build up and improve capacity.

You can easily open up a discussion on smaller slices and faster feedback if you view capacity as a dimension that can be progressively delivered. A solution that provides less capacity often requires simpler versions of components, and might not require some major parts at all. At the same time, it's likely that there are use cases that can be satisfied with less capacity, so even those simpler solutions can be shipped to end-users.

For example, when we launched the first version of MindMup, we wanted to allow users to store documents using our cloud service. This would have required authentication, capacity monitoring, alerts, a database of users, a means of registering and so on – too much to be implemented quickly. We could have launched without all those features, but then anyone with basic knowledge of JavaScript would have been able to see how we uploaded documents, and to abuse our system to store gigabytes of data in the cloud for free. We planned to offer a free service, and letting anyone store any number of huge documents would open us to significant financial risk.

We sliced the product by capacity, and in the first version allowed users to upload only documents smaller than 100KB. This was enough for basic usage, but significantly increased the hassle someone would have to go through to make a financial impact on us by abusing the system. Splitting the work this way allowed us to skip user registration, authentication, creating a database, resetting passwords and most of the other components. Just by limiting the initial capacity, the work required to launch and provide users with some real value was reduced by probably 99%. We then iteratively added elements that would enable us to offer storage of larger documents.

Key benefits

Splitting by capacity can reduce technical complexity significantly for the first release of a product or service, yield valuable feedback early and provide value to some subgroup of users sooner.

Thinking about capacity as a potential dimension of splitting helps to avoid 'all or nothing' plans. Instead of waiting for a few months for all the dependencies to be in place, business users can start providing feedback early. The team can use the learning from lower capacity releases to improve plans and product ideas for higher capacity solutions.

For legacy migrations, splitting releases by capacity allows teams to run both the new and the old system in parallel and migrate use cases progressively to the new system. This is a useful way of de-risking the migration by supporting frequent feedback.

How to make it work

There are many different types of capacity that can be delivered iteratively, so try to consider several dimensions when slicing stories. Some good ideas to start with are:
- file size
- session length
- total number of users
- peak usage (concurrent sessions or data volumes)
- number of items (such as files or resources) available to a single user

Find a dimension where an initial cut would require only a small subset of the final architecture or where components could be significantly simplified. Make sure to check that progressive increase in capacity would require progressive improvement in the architecture and not a complete rewrite.

A dimension that works well for one product or service might not really work for some other context. For example, peak usage or session length wouldn't be a good dimension for splitting MindMup stories because session data is stored client-side, so those things don't really impact architecture that much. On the other hand, session length and peak usage would probably be a great way to slice an online multiplayer game, because a small capacity version could just run on a single machine without any clustering, replication, session sharing or session persistence.

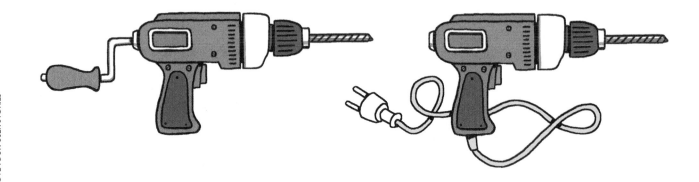

Internal enterprise software is often a spaghetti-like mix of databases, remote services and obscure systems. In such environments, new software rarely works in isolation, and often needs to pull in information from many different places. Making it all work together is a major challenge.

Data-entry screens are often the first focus in any software plan, because data needs to be put in before it gets processed. It's rarely easy to connect to all the relevant reference data sources, so stories involving data-entry screens often get blocked, half-done or postponed. And because teams spend a lot of time perfecting data entry, they can't work on data processing until much later. We've lost count of iteration demonstrations where developers show a beautiful entry screen, and promise that users will eventually be able to use it once someone comes back from holiday and explains how to exactly access relevant product types. Or the entry screen is done and everyone feels great about it, but

nothing actually happens once users put the data in – this comes in later iterations.

The real value of software is mostly in its outputs, not in its inputs. An interesting strategy for splitting stories while preserving most of the value is to avoid any work around preparing inputs at first. This particularly applies to reference data. Instead of loading such data from the official sources dynamically, split the story so that the first part uses hard-coded reference data, and subsequent stories connect the input fields to relevant data sources.

When we worked with a financial services organisation, we applied this approach for a transaction entry screen. There were many good reasons why the list of supported currencies had to be maintained in a single place, but because of slow internal IT procedures we couldn't get access to the main database in time for the first release. Rather than being blocked on that problem and releasing something useless, we agreed with our end-users to temporarily duplicate the data. Our list of currencies was in a text file, which users could easily edit if needed. This significantly simplified the work involved in the first version of a system for entering trades, and allowed users to benefit from the new software sooner. Theoretically, it opened up potential security risks and long term it could create consistency issues, but the first version was released only to a limited number of people who could deal with these concerns through internal business processes. In the third release, we connected the trade entry software to the main database and closed all the risks.

Key benefits

Getting access to the right reference data in enterprise systems is frequently a task that involves more waiting than effective work. Developers often have to wait for authorisation, documentation, and fight with unexpected and undocumented quirks of legacy systems. This is why estimates for such tasks always carry a huge amount of uncertainty and risk. Splitting stories to work with hard-coded data at first improves the predictability of short-term plans and enables development to continue while people wait for access or information.

In scenarios where the reference data is difficult or time-consuming to retrieve, but is unlikely to change frequently, this approach can significantly reduce the work required to put something usable in front of end-users, and let them benefit from the new software.

Even if it's easy to load reference data, but there are many fields on an entry screen, hard-coding the data can help to halve the size of a story. Instead of perfecting data entry, the team can then deal with the data processing early on. This speeds up the delivery of value, and helps to avoid the iteration demonstrations where the only thing to show is a beautiful data-entry screen.

How to make it work

Choosing the right reference fields to hard-code is the key to making this technique work well. Ideal candidates are inputs that would significantly increase effort or uncertainty if they were loaded dynamically, but change infrequently.

Sometimes it's worth asking users to type information in instead of offering a hard-coded list, especially if software is built for internal use and a verbal agreement is enough to prevent exceptions. Examples of such fields are country codes, currencies, titles and so on.

If the data is expected to change frequently, then make it easy to for users to change the reference data. We gave users a text file which they could modify on their own. Another client we worked with applied a similar approach to data entry, and this simplified their deployment so much that they actually created a policy of keeping slow-changing reference data in version-controlled text files rather than in databases.

Lastly, don't forget about the 'then dynamic' part of this approach. Hard-coding reference data is a trade-off between the speed of delivery of value and a potential increase in security and consistency risks. As well as the story that uses hard-coded data, you need some follow-up stories to tidy things up.

SIMPLIFY OUTPUTS

If you've tried to simplify input channels and split by capacity, but a story is still too big, it's often possible to split the story further from the other end, by simplifying outputs.

This approach is particularly applicable to internal enterprise development, where the final output often needs to be stored in an obscure database handled by a completely different team. One of our clients used a complicated legacy data warehouse for reporting, and any changes to that system had to be coordinated across the whole group. They needed to add new reports for accountants to extract tax information from, but instead of doing everything in one story, they choose to save intermediate information into Excel files. Business users had to manually extract tax information from the files, but at least they got to use the new order management features sooner. Follow-up stories automated tax reporting using the data warehouse.

Another situation in which simplifying outputs is effective is where storage introduces significant processing or compliance risk. For example, when working with an online gaming system, we split stories so that initially there was no storage of compliance-sensitive information such as credit card numbers. This

allowed us to push the games out quickly, and deal with payment card storage compliance later. This is a good strategy if the outputs are not needed for critical business reports.

Simplifying outputs is also applicable where outputs are not immediately required. For example, one of our clients had to produce quarterly regulatory reports. We split stories to ensure that the data was preserved but not easily accessible, and later planned stories that would make it easy to access. Effectively, the first few stories produced plain text files, and we later wrote a script to import those files into a reporting engine before the end of the quarter.

Key benefits

For complex enterprise systems, simplifying outputs can significantly de-risk short-term plans. Getting the right access rights and dealing with all the quirks of legacy systems can take up a lot of time, and often involves external people with specialist knowledge or administrative privileges. This is why stories involving external or legacy systems are often blocked and left incomplete. Splitting a story into one that uses a simple output channel and one to translate and push the data forward into legacy systems divides the risk. The first part can be completed while analysts are investigating the second part.

When dealing with complex output formats this way of splitting stories can provide manageable chunks and help teams roll something out quickly instead of working for months on getting all the outputs right.

How to make it work

An easy guideline is to choose one format instead of many formats if possible. For example, if a story involves exporting to PDF and Excel and tab-separated files, divide it into three stories for each output format. Use the first story to process the data and create the simplest output first, then use subsequent stories to provide more format options.

The second good strategy is to store information insecurely first, and make it secure or encrypt it later. This works well in situations where security or encryption is more a long-term concern than an immediate risk. A retail company we worked with had to mask transaction IDs on customer receipts to prevent competitors from analysing their business volume. There was a considerable amount of disagreement about the masking strategy among different business stakeholders, which created a lot of risk for delivery and potentially blocked us from completing end-to-end workflows. The roll-out plan, though, assumed the new software would only be used in one of their smaller shops for a while, which limited the risk. We split stories to avoid any masking initially and used simple sequences at first, then added masking and encryption later. This allowed the client roll out software to the first shop quickly.

The third good strategy is to investigate whether persistent outputs are needed for future data reports or just to improve workflows. If you discover persistent outputs that are not needed for business reports, a good option is to split stories so that the first story handles transient information, and subsequent stories make information persistent. This is particularly useful when data security is an immediate concern, due to compliance or financial risks, since not storing the data postpones all the risks. For example, credit card numbers are often stored so that customer service can process refunds and users can re-order things more easily. Not storing card numbers would slow down workflows, but for most companies it would not have an impact on critical information. Customers would have to enter their card information again for future purchases, or provide account numbers to customer service for refunds. This might be a good price to pay for getting some new features sooner. Not storing order contents, on the other hand, would probably make a huge mess for future reporting, so that wouldn't be a good way of simplifying outputs.

The fourth good strategy is to cut the outputs at a different boundary. For example, use files instead of connecting to the data warehouse. The information is still there, persistent, but just not pushed all the way. The trick with this technique is to create a simplified output that will still bring value. Dividing a story so that the first part creates an intermediate output which end-users don't value is pointless. That would be a technical split, and not a user story. For example, it would be a good idea to split a story to use Excel for reports at first, and then later integrate with a legacy reporting engine, whereas it would be a bad idea to just keep the information in an internal format without sending it on to a place where people can actually use it.

Software development often involves dealing with unknowns. Analysing third-party systems, investigating new standards and assessing the risks of migration to a new version of an infrastructure component are all common tasks. Yet each such task differs from others of the same type enough that people can't really estimate them without digging in and investigating the details.

Stories involving such tasks are almost impossible to plan for effectively. Without knowing at least roughly what needs to be done, nobody can accurately predict how long it will take to implement. Such vague stories often introduce a lot of variability into the delivery process, and the short-term statistical analysis that you would use for regular work won't really apply to planning such stories.

In iterative processes where teams commit at the start of an iteration to deliver stories, such vague stories can lead to nasty surprises towards the end.

Some teams solve this by writing fake user stories, that mostly follow the pattern 'As a developer, I want to understand how the new external API works'. They are rarely expressed in a way that would make them appear as valuable from the perspective of business stakeholders. It's almost impossible to define any kind of acceptance criteria for such stories.

A good way to deal with such situations is to explicitly split the research tasks into a separate story with a goal of its own. A helpful way of thinking about this is that a story should be either about learning or earning. Learning stories help stakeholders plan better. Earning stories help to deliver value to end-users. The big difference between a learning story and a research task is that the story has an explicit goal. The goal should be valuable to a stakeholder and providing enough information so they can make a planning decision. The acceptance criteria for learning stories is easy to specify – you need to work with stakeholders to identify what kind of information they would need in order to approve or reject the work. Then decide how much time the stakeholders want to invest in getting the information – effectively time-boxing the learning story.

Key benefits

Planning for time-boxed learning stories avoids research turning into vague, uncontrolled work that introduces variability. It also removes the need for research outside the regular delivery cycle, preventing long upfront analysis.

Having explicit learning items helps to manage short-term capacity and prevents overloading a team with other stories. This is particularly important for teams who track velocity with numerical story points.

When the learning and earning aspects of stories are split, teams don't have to pretend to estimate learning, or to create user stories with no apparent value. At the same time, this idea also opens up the possibility that the learning ends without a clear conclusion, or even with a decision that implementation would be impractical. This prevents nasty surprises for stakeholders, because a team only commits to the learning story, instead of committing to deliver something vague.

How to make it work

Create a clear time budget for learning stories – how big depends on the importance of the information you're trying to get. This helps you to balance learning stories against earning stories. It will prevent learning-only iterations where nothing useful gets built, and stop the team from spending too much time solving difficult problems that potentially do not need to be solved. If the learning story ends up without a clear solution, the stakeholders can decide if they want to invest more in learning or try an alternative solution.

Get the team to decide on the output of a learning story before starting. What kind of information do stakeholders need for future planning? How much detail and precision do you need to provide? Will a quick-and-dirty prototype be needed to validate a solution with external users, or is a list of key risks and recommendations enough? This ensures that everyone is on the same page and helps you decide who needs to be involved in the research.

Ideally, learning stories should be tackled by cross-functional delivery teams who will later implement the conclusions, not by separate groups. This avoids the need to create documentation, hand work over or transfer knowledge.

Finally, in *Practices For Scaling Lean and Agile Development*, Larman and Vodde warn against treating normal solution design as fake research work, especially if it leads to solution design documentation for other people to implement. They suggest that research tasks should be reserved for 'study far outside the familiar'.

EXTRACT BASIC UTILITY

In situations where a business process has to be implemented in its entirety to be useful, a good option for splitting a story is to simplify the user interaction to the bare minimum. Instead of usability, give users basic utility. The goal is to first make something that enables a user to at least complete a critical task, and then plan for making it faster, easier or require less effort later. Extracting basic utility often involves semi-automated process execution, solutions which require careful use to avoid data inconsistency, or combining tools which require the operator to transfer data between them.

Offering utility instead of usability works best for internal IT delivery, where the end-users work closely with the delivery team. It's much easier to involve internal users in the discussion about the bare minimum interface and support them in semi-automated task execution. The more independent the users are, the more difficult it will be to manage the expectations, so this is not a good strategy for consumer software.

Extracting basic utility is one of the last-resort methods, so be careful to use it only when needed. It is mostly applicable in two situations: when the utility of the underlying business process is questionable, or when there is an urgent business problem that has to be solved and users can survive with a barely usable interface for a while.

Key benefits

This technique works particularly well for splitting a time-critical story into a smaller piece that remains time-critical and a larger section that can be managed without a deadline. Because of this, it is extremely valuable when there is a tight business deadline carrying a significant risk, such as an upcoming regulatory change or expiry of a contract. In situations such as these, extracting basic utility can help to relieve the pressure. If the basic utility part can be shipped on time, the rest can be done later.

Extracting basic utility can also help de-risk larger pieces of work where the underlying business process needs to be tuned or simplified. If you need to first discover what works before making it work well, there isn't much point in investing in neat user interaction until the underlying process is agreed on. For example, we worked with a financial services company that wanted to automate exception ranking to prioritise users' manual tasks. People weren't really sure if this would create the desired outcome or not, so the business stakeholders did not want to invest too much into this area. A simple, quick-and-dirty solution helped to prove the business case and nail down the scope.

How to make it work

When a process is repetitive, the first stage of pairing down to basic utility can be to enable only a single execution. For example, avoid prepopulating information fields and ask users to enter all data each time. Instead of allowing batch orders using a shopping cart, only allow people to purchase one item at a time. As long as security is not compromised, instead of integrating with a legacy system or a third-party channel to load the current status (for example, an account balance), ask users to enter it manually.

The second strategy to extract basic utility is to simplify data entry. Instead of complex user interface widgets, use simple text fields (for example, for dates). Instead of pre-emptive validation on the web page, just reject fields in the back end with a generic message. Instead of formatted WYSIWYG text, support only plain text entry. Instead of providing options for selection, ask users to type values in.

The third common option for extracting utility is to completely change the input channel. For example, instead of users uploading information through a web page, have them load it from a text file. Instead of a queue system that automatically starts a process, ask users to initiate it manually.

Make sure to communicate upfront what you are doing and manage stakeholder expectations. Extracting basic utility is effectively the exact opposite of The Skeleton On Crutches, sacrificing usability for the sake of shipping something quickly. About ten years ago, Gojko led a development team that built a slot machine game and they chose to apply this method of splitting, delivering a working basic game with a horrible user interface. The clients almost cancelled the contract after seeing the first version, even though it was just for internal feedback. It took two months of painful negotiations, with a significant financial risk to the delivery team, to get things back on track. The key problem was that the team did not agree or communicate with stakeholders about the purpose of the first cut.

When stakeholders are aware of the plan upfront, such problems do not happen. For example, we've used this method with a large bank that had to solve a critical reporting problem, and the business stakeholders were amazed that the team could ship something in two days and get the regulators off their back, even though it was borderline usable.

If none of the ideas in this part of the book helps you to break up a larger chunk of work into smaller pieces that would iteratively deliver value, then try the user story hamburger.

The user story hamburger is a facilitation technique that can help teams start to think about value-oriented slices when they are stuck in thinking about technical workflows and all-or-nothing use cases. It is based on user story mapping, but instead of organising many stories into multiple releases, it organises tasks for a single large piece of work into multiple stories. Here is how to create a hamburger:

1. List technical components
2. Define quality attributes
3. List options at different levels of quality
4. Remove unsatisfactory options
5. Remove options that don't produce useful technical slices
6. Choose a slice

First, get the team to list the technical components and the workflow involved in providing the service or the use case that you're breaking down. For example, mailing out an electronic newsletter would involve assembling the list of recipients, sending out emails, retrieving the delivery status for each email, removing recipients of bounced messages and marking successful deliveries. These steps become the vertical layers of the hamburger (think meat, lettuce, tomato...). To make the visual metaphor stronger, draw the half-buns on the top and the bottom.

After the components are in place, define quality attributes for each level separately. For example, quality attributes for assembling the recipient list might be volume and performance. For sending out emails, they might be personalisation, volume and frequency.

For each of the steps, list options that would support different levels of quality. For example, manually sending emails supports very low volumes and infrequent sending. Automated batch sending with some manual setup allows higher volume, but not high frequency. Fully automated setup and sending would offer both high volume and high frequency.

Put the options on the same vertical level as the related technical steps, and order them left to right based on the level of quality. Then as a group evaluate the options in order from the left and discard the ones that won't

provide any useful level of service. For example, sending emails manually might cost too much even for the smallest newsletter, so it should be discarded.

Look at the remaining options and eliminate any that would take approximately the same or more to deliver than options to their right that provide higher quality. These aren't useful slices.

Now that you have a nice hamburger, decide how deep you want to take the first bite. Pretty much any vertical cut of the hamburger should deliver some value to a subgroup of users, so it should be a potentially good start for iterative releases.

After the first slice is delivered, implementing any subsequent option would improve quality at some level. As a team, discuss which step of the process you would like to improve, and select the next option on the list for a story.

Key benefits

The user story hamburger technique helps groups who are accustomed to think about technical workflows and huge use cases to start discussions on multiple options, slices and releases while staying in their comfort zone.

By mapping out options in a two-dimensional table, this technique facilitates a good discussion on opportunities to fulfil the needs of a subgroup of users faster, or to roll out a part of a use case that would still provide value.

By explicitly considering options on different levels of value, the hamburger technique helps teams to consider skipping over some potential components and steps. For example, manually removing rejected email addresses might be an option on the lowest level of quality for marking bounced emails. If a team seriously considers slicing a story to include this option, then they can also consider having a slice without removal of bounced emails. Delivering newsletters without considering previously rejected emails isn't ideal, but it might be perfectly OK for the first two or three weeks of operation.

How to make it work

Keep workflow steps at a high level. Avoid having more than ten steps, otherwise you won't be able to have a decent discussion about options.

When you are collecting ideas, it's best to split the team into several smaller groups and have them work independently, coming together for a joint discussion, similar to diverge and merge.

It's important to explore unsatisfactory levels of quality because this might generate some good ideas, and because the group might discover that it's OK to skip a step. For example, when we worked with a team in a bank on a reporting system, we explored an authentication step, and one of the suggestions was 'no authentication'. This was initially discarded as too risky, but then one of the team members came up with the idea of generating reports and sending them by email to users, which would require no authentication. The number of reports they could set up was low, but it would reduce the technical requirements significantly, in particular because authentication was handled by a team on a different continent. Slicing the hamburger helped this team discover that they could quickly fulfil the needs of their five most important business users, then generalise the solution later.

MANAGING ITERATIVE DELIVERY

There are plenty of things any software team needs to do which just don't fit into user stories conceptually. Within one week, people in a team we recently worked with were involved in setting up new development machines, rebuilding test servers, upgrading to the new version of an infrastructure library, automating test log analysis, and speeding up deployments.

Such tasks aren't stories. They help the delivery team work more efficiently or protect against future risks. All these tasks have an indirect value in that they help the team deliver software more sustainably in the future, but they don't carry any direct value to end-users or stakeholders. Yet for some insane reason, in this particular team all those tasks were turned into fake user stories, written in the typical story format. 'As a

QA in order to test faster I want automated log error reports' is not a user story. It might be in a story format, but unless you are building software for testers (these people were not), there is no good reason why you'd want to capture such tasks as stories.

First, prioritisation of such tasks is pointless. Business stakeholders won't be able to provide any sensible opinion on whether cleaning up a test server is more important than upgrading to the latest jQuery version. Writing such tasks as user stories makes them compete with externally valuable work, and they'll always lose. That is, until the situation becomes unsustainable and the auxiliary work has to get done, in which case the prioritisation becomes doubly pointless.

Second, keeping such tasks in the backlog is also pointless – unless the person in charge of delivery is a statistics-obsessed maniac who wants to account for every working hour. Ultimately, all those tasks translate into work hours and there are much cheaper ways of discovering how many hours there are in a day and how many days there are in a week.

There is a fake argument that it's good to see everything a team does in a single place. But nobody collects stories for tasks such as answering email, reviewing CVs of job applicants, investigating quality issues and so on. From a story planning perspective, tasks such as setting up servers are no different from answering email. They have to happen at some point, and they don't really need to be accounted for any differently.

Lastly, such internally valuable tasks rarely follow the same flow of work as customer-centric stories. There doesn't need to be any formal acceptance criteria, there won't be any meaningful demonstration to stakeholders, and people doing the work mostly know on their own if it was done well.

Managing such tasks as stories just for the sake of it is wasteful and confusing. Please don't do it. The only justifiable reason for mixing such tasks with user stories is to do short-term capacity planning, to find out how much customer-centric work can be taken in. But there is a much simpler solution for this. Just decide upfront. Set a time budget, both an allowance and a limit, and just let the team get on with it. Then discount for that budget in short-term capacity planning.

Key benefits

If the team has a separate, dedicated time budget for incidental work, it can build up slack to deal with unexpected interruptions so that both short-term and long-term planning actually become more accurate. The team also becomes more productive. Instead of wasting time on writing, estimating and managing fake stories, people can focus on getting real work done. This also means that the remaining stories are customer-oriented so teams can have more effective discussions with stakeholders about genuine user needs. Nobody should ever ask a stakeholder about the acceptance criteria for a server clean-up (We've seen this one unfortunately first hand – the answer was spot on: 'that it got cleaned up'.)

A dedicated time for internal tasks helps to avoid competing priorities. Stakeholders are always going to choose externally valuable items over internally valuable tasks, until something internal becomes so urgent that it has to be done. Because of this, most internal work is done as emergency fire-fighting. With a separate allowance for internal work, teams can complete internally valuable tasks at a sustainable pace. This also avoids the need to explain internal work to people who don't care about it.

The budget serves as a limit on the impact of internal tasks to customer-centric work, and ensures that real user stories don't suffer.

How to make it work

Delivery teams should decide on the time budget together with stakeholders and review it periodically. Periodic reviews help to adjust for unexpected business circumstances or technical issues.

There are several ways of spending the budget, and the right one depends on your context. Some teams dedicate a block of time for the entire team, for example the first half-hour of every day, or the last four hours each Friday. Some dedicate a person (or people, depending on the allowance) to handle technical tasks. In *The Art of Agile Development*, Jim Shore advocates having a Batman – a kind of superhero who deals with all interruptions while the rest of the team focuses on customer-centric work. Introducing this role and rotating it to prevent burnout to any single individual was a huge boost to productivity in many teams we worked with over the last few years, mainly because the other team members didn't have to switch context or deal with interruptions.

Don't create two separate backlogs for external and internal items. Every team we ever worked with had a list of things they wanted to do and people knew what these were intuitively. The delivery team can choose the top priority items for internal improvements without a formal tracking mechanism. It's perfectly OK to discuss such items as a group, but full formal backlog management is an overkill.

Detailed estimation works against the whole idea of flexible scope, but many companies we work with fall into a common trap when they insist on work duration estimates. 'We are terrified of uncertainty – we would rather be wrong than uncertain,' said Dan North at Oredev in 2011. A nice precise number feels good, it feels as if someone is in control. The premise of this process is deeply flawed, because all the estimates come with a margin of error that is rarely considered. There are several popular error reduction techniques, such as estimating with intervals of confidence and estimating based on statistical averages, but in many situations this is actually not the right problem to solve.

Long-term estimates give the wrong impression of precision and promote long-term commitment on scope, which eliminates the biggest benefit businesses can get from agile delivery – adaptive planning.

Instead of estimating, try to start with a budget for a bigger piece of work, in terms of both operational costs and time. This budget can then become a design constraint for the delivery team, similar to scalability or performance. Essentially, rather than asking 'how long will it take?', ask 'when do you need this by?' and 'how much can you afford to pay for it?' The delivery team then needs to come up with a solution to fit these constraints. This, of course, requires transparency and trust between the people delivering software and the people paying for it, so it is much easier to do for in-house software than for third-party delivery.

Key benefits

Setting the budget, instead of estimating, eliminates the need to add up smaller estimates, because the final number is already known. This in turn eliminates the need to break down the larger milestone into lots of small stories and analyse them upfront. This prevents wasting time on unnecessary analysis and avoids commitment on scope, and instead establishes a commitment to deliver business value.

Another important benefit is that this approach sets additional design constraints, which enable the delivery team to come up with solutions that fit the business case. A budget makes it clear whether things have to be improvised or should be gold-plated.

How to make it work

The best way to decide on a budget, in terms of both time and money, is to look at the expected business benefit and estimate its value to stakeholders. The financial budget can then be set as a percentage of perceived value, establishing a clear return-on-investment model. One of our clients is a team in a bank working on software which directly reduces the operational costs of financial transactions. The more transaction classes the software could automatically process, the less the bank had to pay people to handle exceptions. When they were setting their budget, they had reasonably good estimates of how many full-time salary equivalents each larger chunk of planned software would save.

Most businesses that we've worked with, unfortunately, are not in a position to come up with a good financial estimate for the value. When there is no good value model, try the following two approaches:
- Ask about extremes
- Budget incrementally

People are often much more comfortable talking about extremes than precise values. Ask about extremes, for example 'What is the least amount of money this has to earn to make any reasonable impact? How much would make everyone say that this was worth it?' This often helps to open a useful discussion. Even orders of magnitude are a good starting point for the discussion. We participated in several workshops where stakeholders decided that the project wasn't realistic after they had quantified the order of magnitude for the extremes. This also works for time constraints. For example, interesting questions to ask are 'How soon could you start using it if it was there already?' and 'What is the latest we can launch this so that you still get some value out of it?'. If the extremes are reasonably close, you can set the target somewhere in the middle.

If they are far apart, then you can aim for the earlier date first, and once that is achieved replan for higher impact at the later date. Any readers with basic knowledge of statistics are by now probably balking at our unscientific suggestions, but remember the context here: companies without a good value model and no prior success at even aligning the expectations.

If the discussion about extremes leads to a dead end, then there is no shared understanding among the stakeholders about the potential value. This often means that things are too uncertain. In such cases, the next step should really be about reducing that uncertainty. Instead of deciding on the entire budget, plan incrementally. First decide on a budget for learning: this can lead to prototypes, low-fi interface testing with users, half-manual processes and skeleton applications, or even business people going back to the drawing board to come up with a shared model of value. The scope of the learning project is often much easier to slice and narrow down, because everyone knows that this will not be the final solution. Once the results of the learning project have reduced uncertainty about the larger target, you can decide to invest in the next step. With less confidence, take smaller steps. With more confidence, take bigger leaps.

A common concern among stakeholders who are using flexible iterative development methods for the first time is the risk of spending the budget but not getting the value. If the value model is relatively linear – meaning that small deliverables can bring value quickly and incrementally – then you can establish smaller milestones and monitor them. For example, after the first 10% or 25% of the budget, review how much actual value was delivered to business stakeholders, and adjust the plan. If the value model is not suitable for this approach, for example when any positive outcome requires a huge investment and there is a lot of uncertainty, then the learning budget approach is a better option.

Story sizing is one of those universal causes of heated debates in online forums, and a stumbling block for many inexperienced teams. Story sizing is useful for one purpose: deciding whether a story is too big to implement or small enough to get fast feedback. Almost any story sizing heuristic can help teams make these decisions. But that's it – story sizes aren't really useful for anything else.

Inexperienced teams often misuse story sizes for long-term planning and capacity management, which is harmful and misleading. It's quite common to see a huge number of stories roughly estimated months before they will even come into delivery, then all those numbers added up to predict when the larger piece of work will finally be delivered. This often turns a rough first estimate into a commitment to finish work on a particular date. The overall number and the resulting date become an anchor for stakeholders and they are used to measure long-term delivery. This commitment on scope and time leads to pressure to follow a pre-determined plan and favours predictability over delivering value. Because unexpected details are discovered only when stories finally come into delivery, teams often end up being pressured to deliver software of insufficient quality. Ultimately, such negative incentives prevent organisations from getting the big benefit of agile delivery – being able to quickly change direction and replan when market opportunities change.

Calculating a long-term estimate based on stories assumes that all planned stories will be delivered and that nothing new will come up during delivery, which completely defeats the purpose of adaptive planning. Even where someone can correctly predict time-to-deliver for all stories, long-term estimates based on stories are horribly misleading unless they are calculated using rigorous statistical methods.

We've never seen a team carefully calculate margins of error or intervals of confidence in their initial story sizes, let alone consider how adding, multiplying and dividing those numbers might affect the overall interval of confidence. Without serious statistical methods, resulting numbers for long-term estimates are worse than pure guesses. The numbers look precise, so they provide a false sense of accuracy and mislead people. The same applies to capacity planning, for example using story points to calculate team velocity. It's useful to know how much work a team can do, but complex arithmetic on approximations misleads and can open up opportunities for horrendous misuse.

When you are comparing stories, try to avoid using numerical sizes. Choose a different sizing mechanism that allows you to make the distinction between 'too big' and 'just right'.

Key benefits

Numeric story sizes often result in tracking progress using the cumulative size of delivered stories, which in effect measures busy work instead of business value. There are much more effective ways of tracking progress and managing short-term capacity and long-term plans than by adding up stories. Unfortunately, numeric story sizes make it too easy for inexperienced teams to fall into bad habits.

Avoiding numbers in story sizes prevents inexperienced managers from misusing them. Not having numbers on stories also forces the team to look for more effective approaches for long-term estimating and capacity planning.

Numeric sizing systems are often unnecessarily complex. We've seen teams waste a lot of time arguing over whether Fibonacci numbers are better than powers

of 2 or pointlessly try to differentiate between stories of size 7 and size 9. Using a simpler sizing method helps teams to go through story planning quickly and make the most important decision based on the size: should a story be broken down further or not.

How to make it work

One good idea is to select several representative stories to serve as a reference, and compare any new stories to them. Again, avoid numerical labels. For example, group stories into small, big and unknown. Many teams use T-shirt sizes, which is also a good approach as long as the number of choices is limited. T-shirt sizing fails when people have to select among XXS, XS, S, M, X, XX, XXX and so on. Limit it to two or three and you'll be fine. The Goldilocks approach also works – pull out stories that are 'too big' and 'too small', and the rest will be 'just right'.

For long-term planning, budgeting is a far superior approach than estimating, but it might be a step too far for many teams. If you have to do estimates due to political or organisational constraints, try to estimate based on average time for a story to be implemented. This works pretty well with a small number of preselected sizes. For example, review the past three months and average out how long it took for a small story to be delivered. It's likely that similar-sized stories will on average take the same time to reach production. Medium-term and long-term planning don't really depend on accurate information for a particular story, but for a group of stories. Averages over a period of time tend to work well when applied to groups of similar stories, because small differences cancel each other out.

Instead of using story points and velocity for capacity planning, try to manage capacity based on analysis time or number of stories.

FIFTY QUICK IDEAS
TO IMPROVE YOUR USER STORIES

104

Teams who work in time-boxed iterations often use story points to calculate velocity, and then plan capacity based on velocity. Although this is good in theory, the approach is prone to misuse and suffers from the same problems with arithmetic as long-term estimation using story points. Unless the estimates are accurate and intervals of confidence are taken into consideration, measuring capacity using previous story points gives precise but widely misleading targets. Even worse, the meaning of numbers changes over time. A story of size 6 today might be much smaller or larger than an average size-6 story several months ago.

Measuring capacity with story points is dangerous because it stimulates the wrong behaviour: cheating to achieve some arbitrary numeric targets. One of our clients worked with a large consultancy that had committed to increasing team productivity – of course measured in story points. As the process changed, the team actually started delivering sooner and better. But story point numbers are all relative and the sizing changed over time. On paper, the team was not improving as fast as expected, so political pressure and contractual obligations got in the way of delivering good software: to increase the number of points, the consultants urged the delivery team to skip testing and deliver half-baked solutions. Immediate problems in the production environment caused stories to come back, but that did not show in project metrics. By the time the consultants completed their engagement, with productivity raised in terms of story points, there were around 1000 defects in the delivered system. Once the consultants left, the delivery team ended up picking up the pieces and having to fight all the production issues.

Capacity planning is important, but velocity based on arbitrary numbers isn't a good way of doing it. Two key aspects of preventing velocity misuse are simplifying the calculation and shortening the time period during which the calculated number is valid.

Averages based on arbitrarily sized stories tend to mislead, but they can be quite effective if all stories have similar sizes. Of course, it's perfectly fine to have different sizes of stories planned for future work – in fact that's the only effective way of managing hierarchical backlogs. But stories coming into the current iteration can and should be of similar size. Try to break larger stories down into similarly sized chunks before considering them for an upcoming iteration. When stories have similar sizes, the averages actually make sense. This means that the average number of stories delivered over the last three to four iterations is a good indicator of how much a team will be able to deliver in the next iteration.

Another typical problem is using velocity for long-term trend management, or for cross-team comparisons. Use this number only for capacity planning, and calculate it based on the rolling average of the previous few iterations. This number will change over time as the product matures and business opportunities change, but it will be more relevant than some absolute number of story points sizes set months ago. Once you only have stories of the same size inside an iteration, the velocity is then simply the count of the accepted stories.

Key benefits

The total number of similarly sized stories is simpler and easier to calculate than an aggregate of some arbitrary numbers. The result will also be more accurate. Small differences in sizes cancel out each other to produce a more accurate final value than applying numerical operations to inaccurate numbers without considering intervals of confidence.

By using a rolling average instead of an absolute number the team can allow for learning during delivery and avoid the negative effects of changes to absolute sizes over time. As the product matures or the team grows or shrinks, a rolling number will only compare capacity to recent events, not the entire history.

How to make it work

Use the rolling average only inside the team for iteration capacity planning. Nobody outside the team needs to know the rolling average.

As consultants, we encountered many Scrum teams who are quite keen on publishing and visualising velocity over time, as a way to show process improvement and track delivered value. This might help to score some political points but it can backfire badly. Velocity is a horribly bad proxy metric for value. Because the meaning of numbers changes over time it's not a good indicator of process improvement over longer periods either. Finding a more direct value metric, such as measuring impacts, is a far better approach.

If you want to publish the number, be careful to communicate the fact that the capacity is a rolling average and does not compare to capacity over longer time periods or across teams. Use the number of stories only for planning the capacity of current work, and not for any kind of long-term commitment – especially not for measuring process improvement.

Avoid using the number of stories for long-term estimates. The average time it takes for a story to go through the pipeline is a far better measurement for long-term planning than any kind of story size.

ESTIMATE CAPACITY BASED ON ANALYSIS TIME

Capacity planning is often an excuse for calculating velocity and requiring story points to be numeric, added up and averaged. In many cases, a simpler solution based on analysis time can be just as good.

In *Practices For Scaling Lean and Agile*, Craig Larman and Bas Vodde suggest that effective Scrum teams spend five to ten percent of each iteration, as a whole team, refining product backlogs. This number corresponds well to our experience. Running specification workshops and discussions on stories typically takes between an afternoon and a day for a two-week iteration. This opens up another possibility for estimating capacity – make it proportional to analysis time. For example, time-box the iteration refinement and planning session and only take into the iteration what you were able to agree on.

For example, a team we recently worked with created a policy to limit the total discussion to three hours, and within that time-box, limit each story to two diverge and merge cycles of 20 minutes each. Allowing for a small break during the three hours, this effectively allows the team to discuss between three and six stories for a two-week iteration. By the end of the first 20-minute block, they expect to get everyone on the same page about the overall scope and to identify key domain modelling questions. If the story is simple and they all think that everyone is clear about what they need to do, the team moves on to the next story. If the team feels that more analysis is needed for the story, they shuffle the teams and analyse the details for another 20 minutes, expecting to identify all the key boundary conditions and open questions. If the delivery team members still think that the story is too vague after the second block, the product owner can choose to split the story or to take it out for detailed analysis. The first option is better if the team was able to agree on a part of the story that would be beneficial to release separately – for example if the main scenarios are clear but exceptions require business clarification. The second option is better if the team was not able to discuss yet, or that they couldn't agree on, the parts of the story that introduce business risk so significant that there is no point in doing anything before clarification. This kind of time-boxing ensures that the team does not get stuck on any particular difficult story, and that the other stories get discussed as well.

Estimating capacity based on analysis time works well in contexts where the critical complexity of delivery is in understanding the business domain. If the majority of your stories are easy to understand from the business perspective, but the tricky part is actually making it work technically or fitting it into an existing legacy infrastructure, analysis time isn't a good indicator. That's why this approach won't work well in contexts where the critical complexity is technical.

Key benefits

Using analysis time as an indicator of complexity is an alternative to measuring story size or counting stories, so it does not require any kind of numeric accuracy. It is also significantly faster than other capacity planning methods. The delivery team plans capacity at the same time as analysing stories, so the time used on guessing numbers can be used for more productive work.

Combined with long-term planning based on cycle time, as suggested in the section on avoiding numeric sizing, this approach to capacity planning removes the need to publish numerical story estimates (or even have them). Because of that, this approach helps teams avoid common problems with using guesswork to enforce long-term commitment.

Limiting the total analysis time also prevents teams from overcommitting. When story details are difficult to nail down, there is a significant amount of risk that the team will discover more unexpected details during delivery. Such stories require more time to discuss initially, meaning that fewer stories are discussed in total, so this approach works well by reducing the number of stories the team commits to in such iterations. In the best-case scenario, the team will complete all the work sooner than expected. In the worst-case scenario, all stories will turn out to be much more complex and won't get completed on time, but at least the stakeholders didn't expect a lot of work to get done in the first place.

How to make it work

Time-box story discussions to avoid a single complex item taking too long. For example, pause a discussion after 30 minutes and see if it's worth continuing with the analysis or not. If the story is too complex, perhaps the examples discussed in the first half hour are a good initial slice. If you couldn't even grasp the story enough to split it in 30 minutes, consider postponing it to the next iteration, so allowing time for more detailed analysis.

Facilitating story discussions with diverge and merge cycles is a great way to get to good results faster, and also provides good time-boxing. For example, if the team is still uncertain about a story after two diverge and merge cycles, consider splitting the story or postponing the work completely.

This approach is most applicable to situations where almost any story can be postponed slightly or split if it is too vague. If you're working in a context where there is no option to postpone stories, it's a good idea to do some analysis a bit ahead of the start of delivery. In organisations where it's difficult to get key business stakeholders to clarify issues and resolve open questions, teams often look into story analysis about two weeks ahead of the intended start of development work on the story. Depending on the typical story complexity, the entire team can get involved or this preparatory task can be delegated to one or two people.

PICK IMPACTS INSTEAD OF PRIORITISING STORIES

Story prioritisation is a classical trap for inexperienced product owners. Those who try to make all priority decisions themselves discover quickly that prioritisation takes too long and nobody is happy at the end. Those who try to delegate priority decisions to business stakeholders find themselves in a cross-fire of people aiming for different business objectives. The problem is often that prioritisation is done at the wrong level.

User stories should be relatively small and provide some value, but a single story rarely delivers everything needed to complete a business objective. Because of this, plans typically include lots of small stories. Such small stories are generally difficult to compare. Unless there is a fire to put out, it will not be easy to choose between a story that saves a bit of call centre time with a new report and a story that reduces fraud by a fraction through tighter payment controls. It's also difficult to decide whether all six stories about fraud reduction need to be done, or if doing just three and moving on to something else after would be better.

As an alternative to story prioritisation, try to pick the most important impacts on customers. Impacts are much easier to discuss and compare than stories, as explained in the section Describe a behaviour change. Combine this with the idea of budgeting instead of estimating and you can get a set of nice constraints for the delivery team. The product owner and the delivery team can then select some stories to fit the budget and focus on working in one particular area until they deliver something visible and usable. Then they move

For situations where the stakeholders already created a huge backlog and there are lots of potential impacts, it might be useful to first prioritise user personae or customer segments, similar to the ideas described in the section Focus milestones on a limited number of user segments. When the stakeholders choose the next customer segment, they can select the next most important impact on those users.

Key benefits

Putting five potential impacts in front of a group of business stakeholders and asking them to choose the most important one is much easier than getting them to look at fifty stories they cannot fully grasp. When the only thing on the table is a bunch of small deliverables, the discussion tends to go towards striking the right balance and giving everyone enough not to complain. When the choice is between reduced fraud and increased payments, the current business situation drives the discussion towards selecting one of them. This enables the team to focus on achieving big business impacts with each release.

Because the number of potential impacts is often an order of magnitude smaller than the count of potential stories, prioritising at a higher level is also much faster. It is also significantly less volatile. If all key decision-makers agree that fraud reduction is currently more important than faster payments, this decision is easier to uphold when someone comes along with a seemingly great product idea that would actually just disrupt

delivery. When the plan is just ten randomly selected stories, it is almost impossible to justify rejecting an arbitrary change. When the priority is set on the level of business impacts, unjustified pet features easily get postponed.

How to make it work

Ideally, select one impact to work on at a time. The question then becomes which of the potential impacts the stakeholders want to achieve first. This will simplify prioritisation: you just need to choose one instead of ranking the list. It will also help you focus everyone on achieving the most important impact quickly.

If you are capable of delivering iteratively (and we assume most people reading this book are), there should be nothing preventing you from doing several small deployments instead of one big release.

As a side note, if your stakeholders aren't pushing you to achieve the most important impact quickly, then it's probably not that important to them, and you should find something more critical to work on.

Make sure that the people who pick the most important impact are actually empowered to make business decisions. Most likely, they will not be any kind of proxy product owner, but the people actually running the business. Raising the level of discussion to impacts will allow you to talk in concepts they understand, so you should be able to get a sound decision. Apart from the fact that choosing impacts pushes business decisions to people who should be making them, getting stakeholders to prioritise impacts ensures that they all know what is coming next. This will prevent unnecessary interruptions and random changes to the plan, while still enabling the business stakeholders to change direction if actual market opportunities change.

MANAGING ITERATIVE DELIVERY

User stories are conversation tokens. Creating a user story is a promise that at some point, the business stakeholders and the delivery team will get together to discuss delivering something in that particular area. The best stories are rough product ideas and survivable experiments, not software features promised upfront. This flexibility and vagueness of stories often results in many more story ideas than a team can deliver in the short term. Organisations with strong product management know when to say 'no', but when there is no strong product vision teams often get in trouble by accepting everything.

A team we recently worked with had eight key business stakeholders in different countries, who were constantly dumping blue-sky ideas into their delivery plan. There was rarely any coordination or business justification for new stories. The product owner was inexperienced and just accepted all the stories proposed by the stakeholders, creating a plan that resembled a stream of consciousness. The team was overloaded with low-level stories and struggled to strike a balance to keep all the stakeholders happy. Unfortunately, because of conflicting priorities, they rarely created any big business benefits. Despite heroic efforts by the team to deliver stories, the business stakeholders perceived that things were moving too slowly. As a result, the stakeholders were constantly changing team priorities, causing a lot of context switching and delaying things even further.

While flexible planning can offer significant business benefits, accepting anything into delivery just because someone thinks it's a good idea can lead to a lot of wasted effort, unnecessary software complexity and high future maintenance costs. It can also create a lot of noise in the plan and delay strategically important deliverables.

If you are working in a situation where it's impossible to refuse requests from senior management, first try to get key stakeholders to prioritise business impacts instead of stories. When someone proposes a change, ask them to review whether the proposal fits the current business objective. If not, offer to stop working on the current objective and prioritise some other impact, or to postpone the proposed change for later. Most of the time, the person asking to change the plan will reconsider. When the new idea is so critical as to invalidate the current business objective, then be agile and replan. When it isn't, the problem will go away by itself. Effectively, never say 'no' – instead say 'not now'.

Key benefits

The key advantage of this approach is reducing interruptions while avoiding political conflict. Saying 'no' might be politically inappropriate, but asking people to accept 'not now' is perfectly fine. Delivery team members will be able to focus on achieving big business impacts and not waste time on ideas anyone from the business can think of.

Introducing a choice between 'now' and 'not now' helps stakeholders with simpler iterative prioritisation.

How to make it work

Create a hierarchical backlog, for example using impact maps or user story maps, to allow stakeholders to prioritise at a higher level before even considering story priorities. This will help to set an overall objective and let people decide more easily if proposed changes actually contribute to it.

A hierarchical backlog will also enable stakeholders to set the acceptance criteria on a higher level, for example on achieving an impact on a customer segment, so it will be easier to decide when to stop working on a group of stories and select a different objective.

The typical pitfall with this approach is that every idea is declared to be critical enough to change the current objective, and we're back to the stream of consciousness. A good way to avoid this pitfall involves two steps:
- Provide a low-friction channel for stakeholders to change direction at regular intervals
- Provide a high-friction channel for someone to push through a critical change between those intervals

For example, set up a product council that meets periodically to review progress on the current objective and to decide whether it should be changed, not on a story level, but on the level of impacts or business objectives. Get an upfront agreement on how the objective can be changed between the meetings, but don't make it too easy.

For teams following Scrum, changing the objective between reviews equates to abandoning the current sprint and restarting. For teams following Kanban, this equates to an expedited class of service. Some teams allocate a fixed number of such changes per year. Other teams require the chief information officer or the managing director to approve each such change. An approach that works well in many situations is to require that a change to the top priority impact between the meetings has to be coordinated and approved by the entire product council.

The two ways of changing the current objective provide everyone visibility over the plan, and an easy way to negotiate changes that are not urgent. As a result, there is typically a lot less pressure from different stakeholders on a delivery team. The ability to switch direction quickly when things really have to change ensures that the business does not suffer in case of an emergency, but the overview of objectives also ensures that the delivery team is not interrupted unnecessarily.

SPLIT UX IMPROVEMENTS FROM CONSISTENCY WORK

User experience (UX) design is one of the most difficult activities to absorb into user stories. It requires experimentation, contact with test user groups, prototyping and frequently proceeds at a completely different pace from product delivery. In addition, software delivery groups rarely have UX expertise in house, so design work is often contracted out to specialist agencies. This all requires UX work to be done well in advance of software implementation, otherwise designers end up just putting lipstick on a pig.

UX improvements don't need small user stories, they need to work at the high level of impacts and behaviour changes. The real challenge here is to discover what is actually needed, and starting with small user stories would require teams to assume a solution. On the other hand, it's dangerous to ignore UX considerations within smaller user stories. Although small stories rarely require serious design work, there is a lot of risk of slowly breaking consistency.

Because of these two different contexts, integrating UX work into regular user story delivery cycles often creates half-baked solutions. For some tasks, designers do not have time to properly investigate and test solutions before developers start implementation work. For other tasks, designers waste time doing obvious stuff, which developers and testers could do on their own with a bit of knowledge transfer.

One solution that works well in many contexts is to divide UX work into ongoing consistency and significant improvements, and manage the two types of work

differently. For ongoing consistency, specialists need to teach developers and testers how to spot and resolve common issues. For larger improvements, designers and developers need to work together in a time box on building prototypes to discover what they actually want to deliver later.

One of our clients creates a mini-team consisting of programmers and designers for UX research, who work on experimental prototypes in a time box separately from the rest of the group. This liberates the mini-team from the constraints of regular work, such as release schedules. Developers can support designers by quickly building prototypes with relevant and realistic data, to flush out any issues with real-world use, while learning at first hand about the key design improvements. The output of the mini-team isn't polished software, it's mostly knowledge about how to give new capabilities to users that should achieve expected impacts. After this stage, the developers from the mini-team go back to the main group and transfer the knowledge, participating in implementing new stories. For maintaining UX consistency, instead of participating in low-level user story iteration work, designers help to create checklists. Developers and testers consider these checklists for each story. Designers also periodically review software to point out potential consistency problems, which helps them to improve the checklists.

Dividing improvement research from ongoing implementation work is a nice example of splitting learning stories from earning stories, on a high level. The time-boxed experimental work can be considered to be a large learning story. Ideally, it will contribute towards a good list of list of lower-level earning stories that a delivery team can confidently implement.

Key benefits

Breaking up improvement research and maintenance of consistency allows teams to work on different levels and avoid wasting time. On the one hand, developers and testers get the low-level information they need in time to build software that provides a great UX. On the other hand, designers don't waste time repeating the same work just because it is needed for each story. They can work ahead of the delivery group, either as part of cross-functional mini-teams or even as a completely separate organisation.

Instead of doing all the work themselves, by creating good checklists and transferring knowledge, designers can avoid becoming bottlenecks. Developers and testers get to learn about UX design, which helps them avoid consistency problems and build better software.

How to make it work

After high-level prioritisation using ideas such as picking key impacts, consider starting with UX research before deciding on user stories. For major changes, it might be worth creating a specialist group to perform customer research, build prototypes and validate them with users before proposing concrete features for implementation. Ideally, involve some delivery team members in the group. If a specialist group is overkill, dedicate a part of the normal delivery team to perform the work. Involving developers will avoid the need for handing information over between teams and prevent an 'us and them' mindset where designers blame developers for not implementing the design solution and developers blame designers for unrealistic and unimplementable designs. Make sure to communicate the expectation that design and prototyping needs to lead quickly to actionable user stories, not to some unrealistic idealistic design documentation.

For ongoing work, involve designers in exploratory testing to detect inconsistencies, then prevent such problems in the future by creating a UX checklist. The checklist does not need to be particularly comprehensive or complex. In fact, complex checklists cause people to avoid them. A good checklist acts as a reminder for people to think, not as a replacement for their brain. For example, asking 'Can it be undone?' is a good replacement for a whole set of items such as 'Warn users about dangerous actions', 'Ask for confirmation before deleting', 'Implement undo on Ctrl+Z for all data changes' and so on.

A good resource for ideas to put in the checklist is the book *Usable Usability* by Eric Reiss. Finally, a fantastic resource on designing good checklists that inspire thinking without overwhelming with information is *The Checklist Manifesto* by Atul Gawande.

GET END-USERS TO OPT IN TO LARGE USER INTERFACE CHANGES

Major user interface changes, such as visual rebranding or significant user interaction redesigns, are a taboo for user stories. It's difficult to get people to discuss small, iterative changes to design. Inconsistent visuals are the closest thing to crime in the design community, so major branding changes have to appear on all web pages at the same time in a big bang.

However, there is a perfectly acceptable way of managing large user interface changes iteratively which avoids all those horrible problems, and even brings a lot of value to designers. And it revolves around simply asking end-users for permission.

In *Inspired*, Marty Cagan writes about using gentle deployment to introduce significant product changes and avoid unpleasant surprises for users. Cagan advises deploying a parallel version of the product and inviting users to try it out at their leisure. Users should be ideally be able to make the new version their default if they like it, but still go back to the old version in case of any issues. After a while, once a large portion of the community has converted, the new version can become the default for everyone and users should be able to opt out and temporarily switch to the old one. Then, with sufficient notice, the old version can be discontinued.

Cagan mostly writes from the context of running a new finished product in parallel with an old one, but such gentle deployment approaches are perfectly applicable for iterative user interface changes as well. In fact, they are commonly used by large internet service providers all the time. At the time when we wrote this, PayPal had a brand new business dashboard that made multi-currency accounts difficult to use. But it allowed users to click on a link to the old interface and manage multiple currencies easily.

Instead of one major upgrade to all your assets, split work into smaller chunks and invite users to opt in to the new interface. Run the old and new versions in parallel, incrementally building up the coverage of the new version. When end-users choose to use the new version, they will be prepared for some temporary inconsistencies and won't mind if one page looks different to the others. New users won't necessarily know about such changes until the whole thing is finished, so there will be no negative impact on the sales funnels or churn. Once the entire redesign is complete, you can make the new version the default and slowly phase out the old version.

As long as the timings are communicated upfront and there is a compelling reason for users to switch interfaces, users won't mind at all. In fact, every time we've done something like this, user feedback on early component redesigns was invaluable and helped us plan the rest of the transition better.

Key benefits

Asking people to opt in reduces the element of surprise. People who explicitly choose to use the new version will be prepared for small inconsistencies – in fact they will look for differences.

If you run the two interfaces side by side, you can divide the large interaction and visual redesign work into chunks and push the new interface into the hands of real users in stages, avoiding the significant risk of a big-bang approach. For example, you can exclude new users from the new interface completely, and only invite experienced users at first.

Finally, by pushing changes to a subgroup of users early, designers can collect feedback on actual use and adjust their designs or the interaction iteratively. For example, when users click the link to switch back to the old interface on PayPal's business dashboard, a questionnaire pops up asking what caused the change.

How to make it work

Provide a compelling reason for people to switch initially. Prioritise the redesign so that the first redesigned component gives some subgroup of users a reason to opt in. Further increments don't need to provide more reasons, but there needs to be at least one good bait. This could be a neat additional feature people have asked for, some new capability that is not available in the old interface, or a solution to a common problem. For a nice example, see the section on splitting stories by examples of usefulness. A compelling reason to change will get people migrating and allow you to collect usage metrics from real use, so that you can improve the design.

Make sure the switch between user interfaces is easy and reversible, so people can try the new one out easily. This will make it appear more as an experiment. As long as users feel that they are in control, you won't get any angry emails.

It's often not easy to support multiple versions of the user interface running in parallel, so the team will have to consider the additional infrastructure work involved in supporting such a staged deployment.

In *Inspired*, Marty Cagan writes that people with a lot of domain expertise often fall into the trap of believing that they can speak for the target customer. This often leads to a false sense of success, over-engineering solutions and, consequently, bad products. Cagan's advice for solving the problem is to test ideas on real customers:

> It is absolutely essential that you test your ideas out with real end-users. It is arguably the single most important part of your job.

In the product management community this advice is mostly taken in the context of working with prototypes. Testing prototypes with real users should ensure that the product ideas that will later become specifications actually make sense. With user stories and frequent iterative delivery, this idea can and should be taken one step further. After a user story is delivered, check that the outcome is as expected with real users.

This was a very painful lesson for us in the first few months of working on MindMup. We aimed to create a highly productive mind mapper with a frictionless interface. Most of our early stories were aimed at increasing productivity. But we never went back to check whether the implemented stories actually made a difference. After reading Cagan's book, we put the idea to the test, and started measuring the actual outcomes. We devised some simple indicators that would be relevant, reliable and comparable over time and for different types of users. If our users were productive, they should have been able to quickly knock up and save simple mind maps – say in less than five minutes. One good metric was the time it took for someone completely new to do this. Then we began to ask how long it was taking for someone to share a map, or even how long it was taking for someone completely new to dive in and start creating a mind map.

Gojko started asking random people at conferences to spend a few minutes doing a quick test, so we could baseline and measure productivity. In the two months that followed, we experimented with many ideas, measuring the outcomes and keeping the ones that actually made a difference. For example, we took the four typical things users wanted to do, and built them into a welcome splash screen for first-time visitors. This reduced the average time to create a new map from almost two minutes to one second. As we repeated the tests and revisited the design and features, we threw a lot of bad ideas out and replaced them with things that actually worked. Novice users were able to complete all the main activities quickly and effectively, and we removed many distractions to reduce friction.

Every book about user stories ever published talks about how good stories need to be testable, but they mostly focus on testing before delivery. Unit tests, acceptance tests, usability tests all prove that the software will deliver the capability for end-users to do something. But there is a huge difference between software providing the capability for something, and the users actually succeeding in doing it. A user story might say that a target customer will be able to do something better or differently, but that doesn't guarantee that users will actually do it. The user needs are often outside the zone of control of the delivery team, but only in the sphere of influence, where they are impacted by other external factors. So even a story that appears to be the best in the world might turn out to be useless due to unknown external factors. To avoid this trap, write user stories so that they are testable for outcome after delivery. And actually go and check with real users that the planned outcomes have materialised.

Key benefits

Even planning to check the outcome after delivering a story makes teams write better stories. It has the same effect as test-driven development does on code. It provides focus and clarity, and leads to better solutions. It stops teams from over-engineering the software.

There are many reasons why expected outcomes do not materialise. The original idea might seem good, but factors beyond our control prevent users from achieving the value. Or the story might be incomplete, requiring a few tweaks. In any case, actually checking the outcome prevents teams from declaring false victories and moving on to new work when they should really be refining existing capabilities. This helps to reduce hidden unfinished features that have been implemented but are effectively incomplete.

How to make it work

The most important aspect of making this work is to plan for checking outcomes during story discussions. A common complaint we hear from product managers is that their user stories can't really be tested in isolation, since there are too many factors influencing outcomes to know if a single feature succeeded or failed. Similar comments are often made about unit testing: developers who work with monolithic systems complain that automated unit testing is not possible in the real world. But when teams write software with automated unit testing in mind, the relevant capabilities are designed in and incredibly complex systems become easy to test. Similarly, when teams write user stories that they intend to check with real users after delivery, they naturally build capabilities to support such testing.

Usage patterns from production systems are often a good first start for measuring outcomes, but they can be misleading as in the MindMup example. Google Analytics only tracked what we explicitly looked for, so unexpected factors didn't show. Watching real people work directly avoids that problem.

If a story failed to deliver the expected outcome, you should discuss with the key stakeholders whether the features should be completed or redesigned and the underlying code changed accordingly, or the code completely removed? Delete failed code if possible, as this reduces future maintenance costs.

If you fear the consequences of removing features after they have appeared in the wild, a good solution is to do staged releases, where only a small percentage of users gets new capabilities. Then rolling back in case of failure is not such a big issue.

Many teams get stuck by using previous stories as documentation. They assign test cases, design diagrams or specifications to stories in digital task-tracking tools. Such tasks become a reference for future regression testing plans or impact analysis. The problem with this approach is that it is unsustainable for even moderately complex products.

A user story can often change several functional aspects of a software system, and the same functionality can be impacted by many stories over a longer period of time. One story might put some feature in, another story might modify it later or take it out completely. In order to understand the current situation, someone has to discover all relevant stories, put them in reverse chronological order, find out about any potential conflicts and changes, and then come up with a complete picture.

Designs, specifications and tests explain how a system works currently – not how it changes over time. Using previous stories as a reference is similar to looking at a history of credit card purchases instead of the current balance to find out how much money is available. It is an error-prone, time-consuming and labour-intensive way of getting important information.

The reason why so many teams fall into this trap is that it isn't immediately visible. Organising tests or specifications by stories makes perfect sense for work in progress, but not so much for documenting things done in the past. It takes a few months of work before this practice really starts to hurt. A story is a token for a conversation. The outcome of that conversation is important even after a story is complete, but it shouldn't necessarily be tied to the story for all eternity. After a story is done, it's better to restructure acceptance criteria by functionality instead of by stories.

Divide work in progress and work already done, and manage specifications, tests and design documents differently for those two groups. Throw user stories away after they are done, tear up the cards, close the tickets, delete the related wiki pages. This way you won't fall into the trap of having to manage documentation as a history of changes. Move the related tests and specifications over to a structure that captures the current behaviour organised from a functional perspective.

Key benefits

Specifications and tests organised by functional areas describe the current behaviour without the need for someone to understand the entire history. This saves a lot of time in future analysis and testing, because even new team members can quickly get up to speed with the project. It is far less error prone too.

If your team is doing any kind of automated testing, the tests are probably already structured according to the current system behaviour and not to a history of changes. Managing the remaining specifications and tests in a similar structure can help avoid a split-brain syndrome where different people work from different sources of truth.

How to make it work

Some teams explicitly divide tests and specifications for work in progress and for existing functionality. This allows them to organise information differently for different purposes. They group work in progress first by the relevant story, and then by functionality. They group tests for existing functionality by feature areas, then functionality. For example, if an enhanced registration story involves users logging in with their Google accounts and making a quick payment through PayPal, those two aspects of a story would be captured by two different tests, grouped under the story in a hierarchy. The team delivering the story can then divide work and assign different parts of that story to different people, but also ensure that they have an overall way of deciding when the story is done. After delivery, the team can move the PayPal payment test to the payments functional area, and merge with any previous PayPal-related tests. The Google Mail integration tests would go to the user management functional area. This would allow the team to discover quickly how a particular payment mechanism works, regardless of how many user stories were involved in delivery.

Other teams keep tests and specifications organised by functional areas only, and use tags to mark items in progress or related to a particular story. They would search by tag to identify all tests related to a story, and configure automated testing tools to execute only tests with a particular story tag, or only tests without the work-in-progress tag. This approach needs less restructuring after a story is done, but requires better tooling support.

Organising tests and specifications in this way allows teams to define different testing policies. For example, if a test in the existing-feature area fails, the team can sound the alarm and break the current build. On the other hand, if a test in the current iteration area fails, that's expected – the team is still building that feature. The significant point is when the whole group of tests for a story passes for the first time.

Some test management tools are great for automation but not so good for publishing information so it can be easily discovered. If you use such a tool, it might be useful to create a visual navigation tool, such as a feature map. Feature maps are hierarchical mind maps of functionality with hyperlinks to relevant documents at each map node. They can help people quickly decide where to put related tests and specifications after a story is done to preserve a consistent structure.

Some teams need to keep a history of changes, for regulatory or auditing purposes. In such cases, adding test plans and documentation to the same version control system as the underlying code is a far more powerful approach than keeping that information in a task-tracking tool. Version control systems automatically track who changed what and when. They also enable you to ensure that the specifications and tests follow the code whenever you create a separate branch or a version for a specific client.

BIBLIOGRAPHY

- Adapt: Why Success Always Starts with Failure, by Tim Harford, ISBN 978-1250007551, Picador 2012
- Agile Testing: A Practical Guide for Testers and Agile Teams, by Lisa Crispin and Janet Gregory, ISBN 978-0321534460, Addison-Wesley Professional 2009
- Anatomy of a Live Music Fan: The Social Effect, BandsInTown 2012
- Beyond Requirements: Analysis with an Agile Mindset, by Kent J. McDonald, ISBN 978-0321834553, Addison-Wesley Professional 2015
- Crystal Clear: A Human-Powered Methodology for Small Teams, by Alistair Cockburn, ISBN 978-0201699470, Addison-Wesley Professional 2004
- Designing for Behavior Change: Applying Psychology and Behavioral Economics, by Stephen Wendel, ISBN 978-1449367626, O'Reilly Media 2013
- Everyman's Prince: A guide to understanding your political problems, by William D Coplin, Michael K. O'Leary and John Vasquez, ISBN 978-0878721092, Duxbury Press 1976
- Explore It!: Reduce Risk and Increase Confidence with Exploratory Testing, by Elisabeth Hendrickson, ISBN 978-1937785024, Pragmatic Bookshelf 2013
- Gamestorming: A Playbook for Innovators, Rulebreakers, and Changemakers, by Dave Gray, Sunni Brown and James Macanufo, ISBN 978-0596804176, O'Reilly Media 2010
- Impact Mapping: Making a big impact with software products and projects, by Gojko Adzic, ISBN 978-0955683640, Provoking Thoughts 2012
- Inspired: How To Create Products Customers Love, by Marty Cagan, ISBN 978-0981690407, SVPG Press 2008
- Lean Analytics: Use Data to Build a Better Startup Faster, by Alistair Croll and Benjamin Yoskovitz, ISBN 978-1449335670, O'Reilly Media 2013
- Practices for Scaling Lean & Agile Development: Large, Multisite, and Offshore Product Development with Large-Scale Scrum, by Craig Larman and Bas Vodde, ISBN 978-0321636409, Addison-Wesley Professional 2010
- Sources of Power: How People Make Decisions, by Gary Klein, ISBN 978-0262611466, The MIT Press 1999
- Specification by Example: How Successful Teams Deliver the Right Software, by Gojko Adzic, ISBN 978-1617290084, Manning Publications 2011
- Stand Back and Deliver: Accelerating Business Agility, by Pollyanna Pixton, Niel Nickolaisen, Todd Little, Kent McDonald, ISBN 978-0321572882, Addison-Wesley Professional 2009
- Switch: How to Change Things When Change Is Hard, by by Chip Heath and Dan Heath, ISBN 978-0385528757, Crown Business 2010
- The Art of Agile Development, by James Shore and Shane Warden, ISBN 978-0596527679, O'Reilly Media 2007
- The Checklist Manifesto: How to Get Things Right, by Atul Gawande, ISBN 978-0805091748, Metropolitan Books 2009
- The Inmates Are Running the Asylum: Why High Tech Products Drive Us Crazy and How to Restore the Sanity, by Alan Cooper, ISBN 978-0672326141, Sams Publishing – Pearson Education 2004

- The Lean Mindset: Ask the Right Questions, by Mary Poppendieck and Tom Poppendieck, ISBN 978-0321896902, Addison-Wesley Professional 2013
- The Learning Alliance: Systems Thinking in Human Resource Development, by Robert O. Brinkerhoff and Stephen J. Gill, ISBN 978-1555427115, Pfeiffer 1994
- The Logical Thinking Process: A Systems Approach to Complex Problem Solving, by H. William Dettmer, ISBN 978-0873897235, Amer Society for Quality 2007
- The Wisdom of Crowds: Why the Many are Smarter Than the Few and How Collective Wisdom Shapes Business, Economics, Society and Nations, by James Surowiecki, ISBN 978-0349116051, Abacus 2005
- Usable Usability: Simple Steps for Making Stuff Better, by Eric Reiss, ISBN 978-1118185476, Wiley 2012
- User Story Mapping: Discover the Whole Story, Build the Right Product, by Jeff Patton, ISBN 978-1491904909, O'Reilly Media 2014
- What Customers Want: Using Outcome-Driven Innovation to Create Breakthrough Products and Services by Anthony Ulwick, ISBN 978-0071408677, McGraw-Hill Professional 2005
- Writing Effective Use Cases, by Alistair Cockburn, ISBN 978-0201702255, Addison-Wesley Professional 2000
- Why the FBI Can't Build a Case Management System, by Jerome Israel, ISSN 0018-9162, IEEE Computer June 2012 (vol. 45 no. 6) pp. 73-80, IEEE Computer Society 2012

Go to **50quickideas.com**
and grab the quick reference
playing cards with all the ideas
described in this book.